THE MORGAN HORSE HEROD.

(*Frontispiece.*)

THE FAMILY HORSE;

ITS STABLING, CARE AND FEEDING.

A PRACTICAL MANUAL FOR HORSE-KEEPERS.

BY
GEORGE A. MARTIN.

1977
Reprint Edition

North River Press, Inc.

Library of Congress Cataloging in Publication Data

Martin, George A   d. 1904.
    The family horse.

    Reprint of the 1895 ed. published by Orange Judd Co.,
New York.
    1. Horses. I. Title.
SF285.3.M37 1977   636.1'08'3   77-3503
ISBN 0-88427-020-3

For additional copies of this volume write to:

North River Press, Inc.
Box 241
Croton-on-Hudson, N.Y. 10520

THE FAMILY HORSE;

ITS STABLING, CARE AND FEEDING.

A PRACTICAL MANUAL FOR HORSE-KEEPERS.

BY
GEORGE A. MARTIN.

ILLUSTRATED.

NEW YORK:
ORANGE JUDD COMPANY,
1895.

PREFACE.

———⋆◦⋆———

OF the thirteen million horses which are estimated to be owned in the United States, fully two millions are kept in cities and villages. All of these, besides many of those classed as farm horses, are purchased after they have attained full growth, and have been broken to harness or saddle. The owners of such horses have no personal interest in questions relating to breeding or early training; but the subsequent care, feeding and management are matters of daily importance to them. It is to meet the wants of such persons that this work was prepared. Breeding and training are not discussed in its pages, but it treats of the daily care, shelter and management of horses, whether kept for work or pleasure. The subject of feeding is examined at some length, both from a scientific and a practical point of view. The horse well merits the most careful, judicious and humane treatment. It is the willing, affectionate servant of man, bearing his burdens and ministering to his pleasure. Yet no other domestic animal is subject to so great and varied an amount of suffering and disability. Nearly, if not quite all, of these are the result of either well-meant ignorance or willful maltreatment. A vast mass of quackery, empiricism and superstition in regard to horse management has become traditional. Much of this is being dispelled through the efforts of enlightened American veterinary practitioners and horse-keepers. This work is in full sympathy with the ideas and practices of such men.

The last four chapters were originally published in the *American Agriculturist*. They were awarded the highest prizes in a competition which drew out more than seventy essays, the examining committee being composed of men recognized as leading authorities in horse matters.

TYPICAL HORSE PORTRAITS.

———•◦•———

HEROD (frontispiece), by King Herod, a son of Sherman Black Hawk, dam by Hill's Black Hawk, son of Justin Morgan. Herod's dam was a daughter of Green Mountain Boy, who was also a son of Justin Morgan. He is one of the most purely bred Morgan stallions now in active service. He was foaled in 1866, and in his eighteen-year-old form made a record of 2:24½.

FRANC TIREUR, page 33, imported French coach stallion. He was bred under the supervision of the French government, from strains which unite the thoroughbred with the Norfolk trotter.

GUY, "the trotting wonder," page 81. Black gelding, sired by Kentucky Prince, a son of Clark Chief, the latter by Mambrino Chief. The dam of Kentucky Prince was Kentucky Queen, an inbred descendant of Justin Morgan. Guy's dam was Flora Gardiner by Seeley's American Star. Guy has a record of 2:12.

COMPETITOR, page 133, imported Cleveland Bay stallion. It is introduced here as a fair typical specimen of that beautiful and useful breed.

(6)

TABLE OF CONTENTS.

THE FAMILY HORSE.

CHAPTER I.

SELECTING THE HORSE.

THE horse is the friend and servant of man, ministering to the pleasure of the opulent and well-to-do, and sharing the labors of the less fortunate. It may be the jaunty road-horse, able to spin along thronged avenues at a gait which leaves rivals behind ; the quiet, steady old favorite of the women and children ; or the faithful, patient drudge which draws a delivery wagon during business hours, and jogs off with the entire family on Sundays or holidays.

In selecting a family horse the first requisite obviously is to keep in view the special use for which it is wanted. The next is to obtain a good horse of its kind. Reliable statisticians estimate the number of horses in the United States at thirteen millions, embracing a wider range of variety than can be found in any other part of the world. Among these the trotter is peculiarly the American horse. It has been brought up to its present high standing by generations of careful breeding and skillful training. But a large proportion of horses from trotting sires are never fitted for the turf, and even with the best training would fail to win success. For a man who loves to indulge in moderate speed, such a horse is admirably well adapted. If it cannot be driven in the magic circle of two-thirty, it can take a road wagon along at an exhilarating gait, and possesses spirit and intelligence which render it a pleasure to drive one.

The Morgans, so popular a few years ago, were the very ideal of a family horse. They were small, though heavy for their height, averaging from fourteen to fifteen hands high, and weighing from nine hundred to a thousand pounds. They were not fast trotters for a mile, but had immense endurance, and would go a long way

(9)

in a day. Every other family of horses crossed with them has been benefited by the cross, and many of the most renowned roadsters of to-day can claim an inheritance of Morgan blood.

The Cleveland Bay has within the last few years become an important element among American horses. It descends from a race which was chiefly bred in the vale of Cleveland, England, and were famous in the old coaching days. The modern Cleveland Bay has been refined by occasional crosses with thoroughbreds. It is a rather long-bodied, rangy, stylish horse, weighing from thirteen to fifteen hundred pounds, deep bay with black points. For moderately heavy work, such as drawing a coupé or a two or three-seated family wagon it is a useful and satisfactory horse. French coach horses are of still more recent introduction to this country. Though bred in France, they originated from crosses of the English Norfolk trotters and thoroughbreds. They are clean-limbed, strong, spirited and moderately speedy. Their importation has made a valuable addition to the stock of American horses. Percheron and other French draft horses have become widely disseminated through the country. They weigh from fifteen to eighteen hundred pounds, and even more; are docile, intelligent, and active for such large horses. Especially are they good walkers, even with a heavy load. Such horses are wholly unsuitable for light driving, but on a suburban place of a few acres one of them is often kept for general purposes. It is used to plow and perform other work in the field, or hitched to a carry-all will trot off with the entire family.

Western ponies have come quite largely into use in the Western and Middle States. Those from the Southwestern plains are called Mustangs, and descend from Spanish horses. They are from thirteen and a half to fourteen hands high, and weigh from eight hundred to nine hundred pounds. A very usual color is a yellowish dun or "buckskin," with a dark stripe down the back. They are active and spirited, and if they have been long held in captivity, are likely to be tricky. But this is due more to the savage manner in which they are "broken" and used, than to any inherent viciousness. If treated kindly from the first, they are docile, useful little animals for light family work. The Indian pony or "Cayuse," which comes from the Northwest, is hardier and ordinarily less spirited than the Mustang. Both kinds have the substantial advantage of cheapness. There are dealers who buy up large droves of them from first hands, bring them east, and sell them at comparatively low prices.

It is not to be supposed that any set of rules can be laid down, which will enable a person wholly unfamiliar with horses to select one, relying entirely on his own judgment. It is always desirable to buy of a reliable person in whom the purchaser can have confidence. If this is out of the question, it is well to have an experienced and reliable friend who will assist in the purchase.   Still, no one is

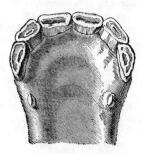

Fig. 1.—THREE YEARS.   Fig. 2.—FOUR YEARS.

willing to leave such a matter blindly and wholly to a third person, even though it may be an honest seller or a faithful friend. Any person who knows enough about horses to keep one, prefers to use his own judgment to some extent at least, in selecting a horse.

THE TEETH.—The first and one of the most important points to be determined is that of age. This is indicated in many ways, but one of the most marked and reliable signs is found in the appearance of the teeth. There are two sets of these—the milk teeth, which

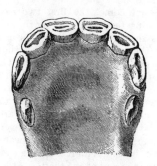
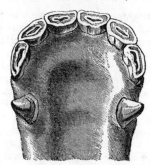

Fig. 3.—FIVE YEARS.   Fig. 4.—SIX YEARS.

are the first to appear, and the permanent set which gradually replace them, the change being completed at the age of five years. A horse has forty teeth in both jaws, but it is the incisors or front teeth of the lower jaw which are usually examined to ascertain the age. There are six of these. They are covered by a fine white enamel enclosing the dentine or bony substance of the tooth. In each permanent incisor, when it first appears, is a large cavity or pouch, extending about one-third of the length from the crown. This cavity is lined with enamel, and the lower part is filled with a dark cement. The incisors or cutting teeth, when new, are oval near the summit, and nearly triangular towards the roots. The teeth of a horse usually wear down at the rate of about one-twelfth of an inch a year. As this wear goes on, the exposed summits of the teeth present different aspects from year to year. The accompanying illustrations, after Thomas Brown, show these changes in the incisors of the lower jaw. At three years old the two front milk teeth have been replaced by permanent ones, with the peculiar hollow in the summit called the "mark." The canine teeth or "tushes," as horsemen call them, are just showing beneath the gum. At four

Fig. 5.—SEVEN YEARS.   Fig. 6.—EIGHT YEARS.

years two more permanent teeth have come, the first two have become somewhat worn, and the canine teeth are coming through the gums. When the horse attains the age of five years, the permanent incisors are all in place; the two "corner teeth" show the mark very distinctly, while it is entirely worn off from the two middle incisors and partly off from the next two. At six years the outer edges of the corner teeth are worn down, and the mark is nearly obliterated from the two next ones. At seven years the edges of the corner teeth are still more worn, the mark is nearly gone from the middle of each, and the four front ones are worn down entirely smooth. At eight years the mark has disappeared from all the nippers. The dark spot in the center is a long oval, lined with enamel, which comes near the front of the tooth. At ten years the marks have worn entirely off the upper incisors, the dark spot in the middle is smaller, and the four in front are less regularly oval. At twelve years the enamel has nearly disappeared from the central spots in the lower teeth, the four in front are somewhat triangular in form. At fourteen years the four front teeth have become decidedly triangular, and the corner teeth partially so. At seventeen years the lower nippers are all triangular, and the four

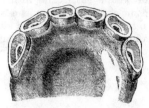
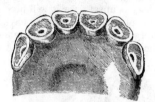

Fig. 7.—TEN YEARS.   Fig. 8.—TWELVE YEARS.

front ones very long from front to rear. The central enamel has all disappeared from the upper nippers, and the "tushes" point forward. From this time on the teeth continue to become flattened from side to side, and longer from front to rear. Another mark of age is the angular protrusion of the front teeth, which increases rapidly after the eighteenth year. The teeth are sometimes manipulated by unprincipled dealers in a manner called "bishoping," with intent to deceive. But the trick is easily detected by close examination. Where the cavity or mark in the center of a tooth is artificially produced, it will have no enamel lining, but instead will show the raw dentine inside. The gums of old horses shrink away, the under lip hangs down.

For ordinary light driving four years is old enough to begin with, but where heavy or regular work is required, the horse should

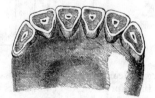

Fig. 9.—FOURTEEN YEARS.   Fig. 10.—SEVENTEEN YEARS.

not be less than six years. There is clearly an advantage in buying young horses, as they increase in value for several years, while those which have passed their prime deteriorate in a still more rapid ratio.

Whatever may be the age or breed, it is essential that the horse should possess a sound constitution, correct form, intelligence and good temper. A narrow browed or Roman nosed horse with evil temper is undesirable, however many good points it may have in speed, age or shape. A horse naturally gentle but lacking in intelligence is unsafe, for it will become panic-stricken and lose its head. Some of the quietest horses have been known to run away and kick things to pieces from fright, when an intelligent animal would have seen nothing to excite panic. A stupid horse will never show affec-

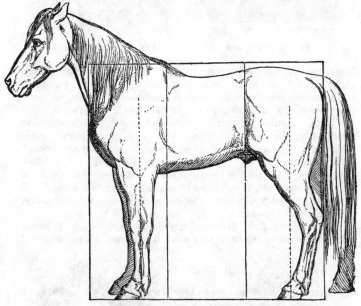

Fig. 11.—SIDE VIEW OF HORSE.

tion or learn anything. The best index of a horse's mental capacity is the expression and color of its eyes. Any considerable amount of visible white is undesirable. A broad full forehead generally indicates a good brain. Of course these signs are not infallible ; a horse may have a very attractive appearance and yet have vicious tricks by inheritance or from previous bad management. The writer once bought on trial a beautiful chestnut mare, which proved to be kind, intelligent and affectionate, in fact a very model of a family horse, until one day when a stranger attempted to drive her with a little more than the usual load. The driver yelled at the mare as she was going up hill, and she immediately balked. The loud angry tone had brought out a latent disposition to balk which she had acquired from overloading and unkind treatment in her fillyhood. So she was voted a failure and returned to the dealer.

The neck should be reasonably long and arched, rather light where it joins the head. A bull-necked horse is clumsy and hard-bitted, and a ewe-necked one is weak and a star-gazer. The chest should be deep and round, with ribs well sprung, giving plenty of room for the heart and other viscera; the shoulder high in the

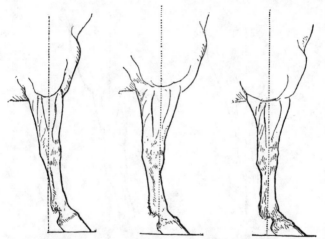

Fig. 12.—STRADDLED. Fig. 13.—" SHEEP-KNEED." Fig. 14.—WEAK PASTERN.

withers and sloping; the upper arm powerful and muscular; the shank short, lean, not beefy, with round sinews and flat bone; the pasterns not too long, but oblique; the hoofs round, free from grooves running up and down. The back should be short between the withers and the croup; the loins broad and muscular; the quarters powerful and solid; the hocks large, bony, and well set down; the shanks strong, flat and clean.

Mrs. M. L. Knowles of Michigan, who owns and personally conducts a successful stock farm, briefly describes a good horse as follows: "Shakspeare describes a horse as 'Round-hoofed, short-jointed, fetlocks shag and long.' Never mind the long fetlocks, good breeding is indicated by short ones; but be sure it has sound hoofs of fair size and good frogs and broad heels. 'No frog, no foot ; no foot, no horse.' The pasterns should be short, with round, smooth joints, good-size cannon bone, also short, with clean-cut ligaments and strong tendons, good-sized knee, and hocks clean and bony, long forearm, and from point of hip to hock ; stifles wide apart ; broad and muscular hips, a well-muscled and slightly-arched loin, short back, sound barrel, deep girth and oblique shoulders, a broad chest and nicely arched neck, fine at the throat-latch, and a head of the good old Morgan type. Such a horse is a model, with docile and tractable temperament, resolution, power of endurance, and pleas-

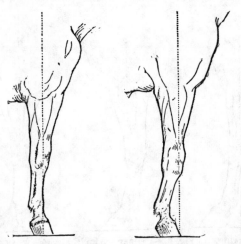

Fig. 15.—STRAIGHT HOOF.   Fig. 16.—KNEE-SPRUNG.

ing appearance, It has a prominent eye, wide forehead, broad jowls, fine muzzle, and nicely-shaped ears."

FEET AND LEGS.—But the points in a horse upon which everything else literally rests, are good feet and legs. Without them, the best breeding, the most perfectly formed head and body, are of no avail. The illustrations, figs. 11 to 23, after drawings by H. M. Hartmann, show the right and wrong kinds of legs and feet. Figure 11 shows the horse from a side view. The legs and body of a horse of average normal shape just fill a square, formed by a horizontal line drawn from the top of the wethers, and another at the bottom of the feet, and vertical lines from the front and rear. If this square is divided into three equal parts by vertical lines, one of them will fall at the point of the shoulder-blade, and the other at the point of the hips. The dotted lines show that the fore-feet stand directly under the joints of the shoulder, and the hind feet under the hip-joint. The off hind foot is shown thrown out of this line. The next five engravings show the fore-legs in false positions, as viewed from the side. When one of the fore-feet is kept forward,

as in figure 12, it indicates navicular disease, one of the worst and most incurable ailments that can affect a horse's foot. If both the fore-feet are held in that position, it justifies a suspicion that the horse has some time been foundered. Figure 13 shows a " sheep-kneed " fore-leg, and figure 14 a pastern too long and oblique. Figure 15 shows a hoof too straight and the foot brought under the body. Figure 16 is a knee-sprung leg. When a horse stands with all its legs tucked under its body, it has been quite knocked to pieces by abuse and hard work. Figure 17 is a pair of correct fore-legs and feet, viewed from the front. They are well spread apart at the breast, the feet point directly forward, and the whole leg is set vertically under the shoulder-joint. Figure 18 shows a bad pair of fore-legs, which accompany a narrow chest and weak constitution. Figure 19 shows a similarly contracted chest and knock-knees. The inner sides of such feet wear off more rapidly than the

Fig. 17.—GOOD FORE-LEGS.

outside, and the whole conformation is weak and objectionable. The " pigeon-toed " feet, figure 20, are equally bad. They are sure to interfere, or cut the leg with the other, and no manner of shoeing can overcome this difficulty. Figure 21 shows a pair of perfect hind legs. A line falling from the level of the hip joints, would intersect the hocks and heels. Figure 22 shows a pair of " cow-hocked ' hind legs, and figure 23 a pair of hind legs, with the feet shaped so that the greater part of the wear comes on the outside, the hocks straddle outwardly. With the feet straight on the ground, this is no

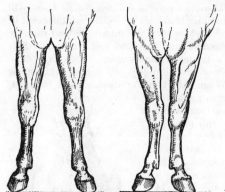

Fig. 18.—STRADDLED.   Fig. 19.—KNOCK-KNEED.   Fig. 20.—PIGEON-TOED.

defect, if hard pulling is required. It has an awkward appearance, however, and is a serious fault in a carriage or saddle-horse.

Here are some valuable hints by the late Col. M. C. Weld on good and bad legs: "All the training in the world will not give a horse good legs, and with this wanting, the spirit and the sort of style which is developed by training and oats, counts in real work and service for very little. A horse needs both, and then there is some hope for him. With a good set of legs the trainer has the right foundation to build upon. It is quite a 'point,' as they say 'on the street,' to know good legs when you see them. It does not take an expert to tell if a set of legs look all right from the side, when the horse is either still or in action, but the real points of view to judge critically are directly in front or behind. The feet are round, well up at the heels, large, solid, and free from either grooves and ridges running up and down, or from irregularity in the lines of growth, which always form fine parallel striæ

Fig. 21.—GOOD HIND LEGS.

in a healthy hoof. It is a suspicious circumstance if these are filed off and the hoof made smooth. The fact is, nothing is a surer index of previous good health than the hoof. If a horse has a fit of sickness the hoofs cease growing, and when they begin again with returning health they all show a ridge; so if from any cause one foot is affected by fever, or a wound, it alone will show it almost certainly by increased or decreased growth, as the case may be.

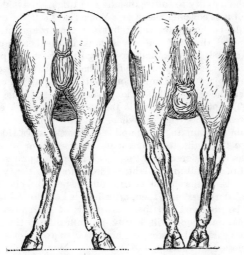

Fig. 22.—COW-HOCKED.   Fig. 23.—BOW LEGS.

The joints are large, hard, bony, and free from meat or puffs. Below the hocks and knees the bone of the leg is flat, and of good size for the weight of the animal; the cords are hard as bone, free from muscle, and the skin free from scars and drawn tightly over the whole. Avoid slender pasterns. The pastern bones and those forming the pedal joint should have all the breadth and solidity possible. The muscular portion of the legs—the fore arms and thighs—should be large and even, and the muscles should stand out individually distinct and hard."

UNSOUNDNESS AND BLEMISHES.—It is impossible to detect with certainty all the diseases and various forms of unsoundness to which a horse is liable. Unsoundness has been judicially defined as "an infirmity which renders the horse less fit for immediate use than he otherwise would be, and less able to perform the proper and ordinary labor of a horse," (Robert *vs.* Jenkins, 21 New Hamp., 116). There are blemishes which do not come under this definition, but are more or less plainly visible, and vices which also impair the value of the horse, but are generally found out after the horse has been used. It is always best in buying a horse to insist on a general warranty that it is "sound and free from vice and blemish." Yet there are many kinds of unsoundness, which may be detected by care and observation, and the liability to future dispute and litigation avoided.

We will first consider the eyes. Youatt says : " The eye of the horse should be large, somewhat but not too prominent, and the eyelid fine and thin. If the eye is sunk in the head, apparently little, and the lid is thick, and especially if there is any puckering towards the inner corner of the lids, that eye is diseased or has lately been subject to inflammation ; and particularly if one eye is smaller than the other, it has at no great distance of time been inflamed." The pupil of the eye is the dark center, black except in white or cream-colored horses, where it is red. The iris is the colored portion surrounding the pupil. In healthy eyes this is very sensitive to the light, its movements contracting or dilating the pupil, as the light is greater or less. It is a common practice to lead a horse out of its stall to the light, before examining the eyes. This is wrong. The pupils should be carefully inspected while the horse is in partial darkness, and then, after it is led out to the full light, it should be observed whether the pupils of both eyes contract equally. A blind horse will betray its infirmity by the incessant motion of its ears, and by stepping high, as if to avoid some obstacle. If, upon close examination, the crystalline lens, which is in the front of the eye, exhibits a cloudy or pearly appearance, or shows a minute spot in the center, cataract and complete blindness are likely to ensue.

Catarrh shows itself in a slight and irregular discharge from the nostrils, and weeping from the eyes, and in aggravated cases with sore throat and cough. It is an unsoundness, but curable. In epizoötic catarrh the discharge is greenish. Glanders, a loathsome, incurable disease, fatal alike to man and beast, is marked in its first stages by a thin, watery discharge from one or both nostrils. In more advanced cases the discharge is glairy and sticky. It is generally the safest to look with suspicion on a horse with any discharge from the nostrils. Roaring is a loud grunting sound produced by the act of drawing in the breath. It may be detected by trotting the horse briskly for a few rods, hurrying it up a hill, or threatening to strike it. Heaves or broken wind is readily observed by the manner of breathing. The inspirations are somewhat hurried and the expirations are accompanied with a peculiar bellows-like heaving of the flanks, particularly after rapid or violent exertion. It is an unsoundness, and can never be cured.

Crib-biting, or cribbing, is a vicious habit, which greatly impairs the value of a horse. It consists of seizing the manger or any object within reach by the teeth, violently extending the neck, and then, with a grunt, sucking in air. It has long been a disputed point whether the habit of cribbing alone constitutes legal unsoundness,

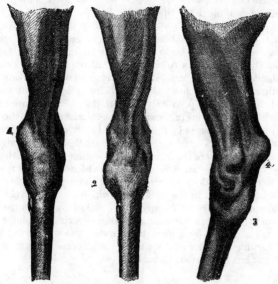

Fig. 24.—1, THOROUGHPIN; 2, SPAVIN; 3, CURB; 4, CAPPED HOCK.

but it is unquestionably a serious vice. The effects of the habit are plainly seen in the condition of the front teeth. The outer angles will be found to be rounded off, and in a horse which has long indulged the habit the front teeth are greatly worn down.

Broken knees are caused by falling. If the knees show white spots or extensive scars, it is never safe to buy the horse as sound. A horse which has gone down once and wounded its knees so seriously as to leave scars, is liable to do it again. Navicular disease is located in the lower part of the foot, and shows itself by lameness, which often disappears after the horse has gone half an hour or so. It is also the actual seat of many supposed diseases of the chest and shoulders. Thrush is marked by an offensive discharge from the cleft of the frog, which may readily be seen by lifting and examining the foot. Quittor is a suppurated condition of the foot, which often manifests itself by a discharge of pus through an opening immediately above the hoof. Ringbone is a bony deposit on one of the pasterns near the joint. Windgalls are little sacs on the fore or hind legs, wherever the tendons are exposed to pressure or friction. They may be detected by passing the hand carefully down the leg. Splints are bony tumors, which appear on various parts of the shank bone. They do not always cause unsoundness, but are blemishes. The hocks are subject to various troubles, which should be looked for in buying a horse. A thoroughpin (1, figure 24) is a round swelling above the hock, similar to a windgall. Curb (3, figure 24) is an enlargement at the back of the hock, three or four inches below the point. Horses that are cowhocked (figure 22) are peculiarly liable to this. Spavins are of various kinds. Bog spavins (2, figure 24) are enlargements on the inside of the hock joint, caused by the escape of the synovial or lubricating fluid of the joint. Youatt very aptly defines them as "windgalls of the hock." Blood spavin is a similar swelling, filled with extravasated blood. They are serious defects, which greatly impair the value of a horse. Bone spavin is a still more formidable disease, being a bony deposit in the hock joint, which destroys its elasticity, and quite unfits the horse for anything but slow work. Capped hock (4, figure 24) is a soft fluctuating tumor, covering the outer point of the hock, caused by a hard blow, a concussion received in the act of kicking, or other cause. It does not necessarily produce unsoundness, but is a serious blemish.

CHAPTER II.

FEEDING AND WATERING.

THE health of the horse, and its ability to perform the service required of it, depend to a large extent upon proper feeding. A great amount of suffering and disease is doubtless caused by bad food, or neglect of correct method. The horse has relatively the smallest stomach in proportion to its bulk and weight of any domestic animal. The liver of a horse has no gall-bladder, the bile being secreted and supplied during the digestive process. The entire anatomy and physiology of its digestive apparatus show that the food of the horse should be nutritious in quality, supplied frequently, and in comparatively small quantities. The food, of whatever kind, must of course be of good quality, sound and wholesome; but beyond this no specific rules can be laid down for general application. The amount and character of the food must vary with the size and constitution of the horse, the climate and season, the amount of work required, and the country it lives in. The horse is an inhabitant of nearly all parts of the earth, and exhibits a wonderful adaptability to various situations. In Arabia its principal food is barley, varied by scant herbage, and even dates; in Iceland and some of the Shetland Islands it subsists mainly on dried fish. The author once saw a diminutive pony, which had recently arrived from one of the smallest and bleakest of the Shetland Islands. Its food had consisted almost entirely of dried fish, a supply of which was necessarily brought along with the pony to avoid too abrupt a change to other food. It was interesting to observe the puzzled expression of the shaggy little beast, as it watched its new companions nipping the grass. On the western plains great herds of horses retain splendid health and vigor through the rigid and stormy winters, upon the dried bunch grass, often having to paw away the snow to reach it. In England the food of horses is mainly hay, oats and beans, (the last named is the broad flat *Vicia fava*, and not the kidney bean); while in various parts of the continent, horses are fed on rye, barley, and inferior qualities of wheat. In India the common food of horses is a plant of the pea family (*Cicer arietinum*), known by the local name of "gram." In some parts of the United States and southern regions of Europe Indian corn forms an important element in horse food, but not to such an extent that "American horses rarely taste oats," as is asserted by an eminent English author. Good, well-made hay, free from dust and dirt, and sound, well seasoned oats may, in a general way be regarded as the staple food for horses. But no animal can do as well on a monotonous diet, even if of good quality, as it will with a judicious variety. Careful analyses have been made of the various food products, and their respective chemical constituents ascertained, approximately at least. It is well known that certain food elements, consisting largely of carbon, produce fat and heat. These are commonly known as carbohydrates. Another class, rich in nitrogen, and known as albuminoids, are mainly muscle formers. The following table exhibits the nutritive constituents of various kinds of food material, as determined by Dr. Peter Collier of the U. S. Department of Agriculture, and Dr. Wolff, of Hohenheim, Germany:

KIND OF FOOD MATERIAL.	Albuminoids.	Crude Fibre.	Other Carbohydrates.	Fat.	DIGESTIBLE NUTRIENTS.			Nutritive Ratio.
					Albuminoids.	Carbohydrates.	Fat.	
Timothy Hay	9.7	22.7	45.8	3.0	5.8	43.4	1.4	8 : 1
Hungarian	10.8	29.4	38.5	2.2	6.1	41.0	0.9	7 : 1
Red Clover Hay	12.3	26.0	38.2	2.2	7.0	38.1	1.2	1 : 3
Alfalfa Hay	14.4	33.0	27.9	2.5	9.4	28.3	1.0	2 : 8
Corn Fodder	1.1	4.1	6.5	2.0	3.2	43.4	1.9	14 : 4
Esparsette (green)	3.2	6.5	8.2	0.6	2.1	8.0	0.3	4 : 1
Corn Stalks (green)	1.8	4.4	9.3	0.5	1.0	8.4	0.2	9 : 1
Wheat Straw	3.0	40.0	36.9	1.2	0.8	35.6	0.4	45 : 8
Oat Straw	4.0	39.5	36.2	2.0	1.4	41.1	0.7	29 : 9
Oats	12.0	9.3	55.7	6.0	9.0	43.3	4.7	6 : 1
Indian Corn	10.0	5.5	62.1	6.5	8.4	60.6	4.8	8 : 6
Barley	10.0	7.1	63.9	2.5	8.0	58.9	1.7	7 : 9
Wheat Bran (coarse)	12.9	8.1	59.1	3.5	10.0	48.5	3.1	5 : 6
Linseed Cake (new process)	32.4	7.3	31.5	3.6	27.6	27.0	3.2	4 : 1
Cotton-seed Meal	41.5	24.4	3.1	18.0	33.2	17.6	16.2	1 : 8
Carrots	1.0	1.4	10.8	0.2	1.4	12.5	0.2	9 : 3

The figures under the head of "Nutritive Ratio" in the last column represent the relative proportions of carbohydrates, or elements that supply heat and fat, and the albuminoids or muscle-forming elements. The actual per cent of digestible nutrients in any kind of food product varies greatly, but the ratio remains substantially unchanged.

An improved method of presenting the facts at a single glance is the following diagram, prepared by E. H. Jenkins, Ph. D., of the

Connecticut Experiment Station. It shows the average quantities of albuminoids, fat, nitrogen-free extract (or carbohydrates), fiber, ash and water which have been found by analysis in alll our common feeding stuffs. Each band in the diagram represents one hun-

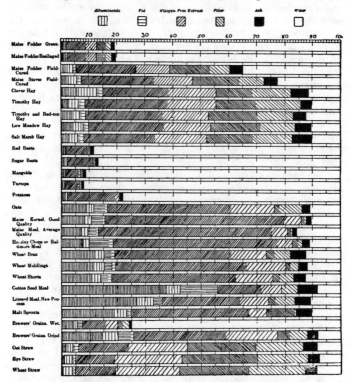

[The part of each of the first four elements that is digestible is indicated by the close shading; the more open lines show the proportion that is not digested.]

Fig. 25.—APPROXIMATE VALUE OF VARIOUS STUFFS.

dred pounds or one hundred per cent of the feed named in the margin on the left. The proportional quantity of each food ingredient which makes up this hundred pounds is shown in the way indicated above the plate. Thus the massed perpendicular lines denote albuminoids ; horizontal lines, fat; oblique lines, running downward toward the left, denote nitrogen-free extract ; while oblique lines running downward to the right denote fiber. Mineral matter or ash is printed solid black, and water has no marking at all. These statements of composition are derived wholly from analyses made in the country, chiefly at our agricultural colleges and experiment stations, and are taken from the tables annually published by the Connecticut Experiment Station. A glance at the diagram will show the composition of any of the food substances named. If precise figures are required, they may readily be read off on the scale at the top of the plate. A single division represents one pound in one hundred or one per cent. A pair of dividers or a fine rule will be a great help in this measurement.

In the second place the diagram shows what part of each of the food ingredients is digestible. No feeding stuff is wholly digestible. A certain part of any feed passes through the animal unchanged. The quantity of this indigestible matter is quite different in different feeds. For instance, nearly nine-tenths of the albuminoids of cotton seed meal are digestible, while of the albuminoids in hay of poor quality only about one-half are digestible. The proportion of each is presented to the eye in the diagram as follows : A portion on the left side of each space representing either albuminoids, fat, nitrogen-free extract or fiber is darker shaded than the rest of the space. This shaded portion indicates both the proportion and the real quantity of the food ingredient which is digestible. To illustrate, cotton seed meal has 42.4 per cent (or pounds in the hundred) of albuminoids, but the diagram shows that 37.6 pounds only are digestible and have feeding value. Only a few digestion experiments have been made in this country yet, so that the figures for digestibility given by German authorities have necessarily been used in most cases. The results of American observation have been used so far as they were available. It must be understood that this chart represents averages ; it is a general statement. All feeds vary more or less—some of them widely—in composition according to differences of soil, climate and season in which they were grown. Animals, too, differ considerably in their powers of assimilating food. Horses digest a smaller proportion of crude fiber than sheep or oxen. Still the diagram is valuable in presenting to the eye at a glance a comparative statement of the average composition and nutritive value of our feeds. It embraces in addition to the articles named in the preceding table, a large number of articles that are not usually fed to horses, but is nevertheless valuable for general reference.

With the results of skillful chemical analysis before him, the feeder need no longer proceed in a haphazard manner, or follow blindly in old ruts, often buying at heavy cost certain standard kinds of food, when equally valuable material of other kinds is cheap and plenty. He has only to adjust the rations in such a manner that they will contain about the correct proportions of the various elements. Those proportions should be varied according to the season. the amount of work required, and the constitution of the horse. In estimating the nutritive ratio of any food, the amount of "fat" is multiplied by two and four-tenths (2.4), and the amount added to the other carbohydrates.

TIMOTHY HAY with oats, as remarked above, may well be regarded in this country as the standard article for feeding horses. But there are many other grasses equally available. In the prairie regions and farther west there are several species of blue-joint and other wild grasses scarcely inferior to timothy. Some of these attain immense growth in rich bottoms, and if cut at the right time, and properly made into hay, are both palatable and wholesome for horses. The Muhlenberg grass (*Muhlenbergia glomerata*), which is found in moist situations, is eagerly sought by horses, and is superior in nutritive value to timothy, either green or as hay. There is a false impression among some horse-keepers that hay, like wine, improves by age. On the contrary, careful experiments show that hay which has been kept more than a year, loses 12.29 per cent of its digestible albuminoids.

HUNGARIAN GRASS and GERMAN MILLET, if cut and cured just as the first blossoms appear, make a hay scarcely inferior to timothy.

CLOVER and ALFALFA are rich in albuminoids. Either one makes a well-balanced ration with corn-meal, corn-fodder, straw, or other material containing an excess of carbohydrates. Esparsette is another name for sainfoin, which has quite recently been cultivated to some extent in Utah, and other parts of the region west of the 100th meridian. It will grow in soils containing lime, even if too dry for alfalfa. It contains a greater proportion of nitrogenous elements than clover or alfalfa.

CORN FODDER is a better feed for horses than is generally supposed. But it must be bright and well-cured. If allowed to stand for months in small stooks, with the butts on the soft ground, and the tops and leaves exposed to the weather, it is unfit for fodder. On the other hand, if stored away while damp in a barn loft, and allowed to mould and rot, it is not only unpalatable, but actually pernicious to the health of animals which are compelled to eat it. "Fodder corn," which is raised expressly for the leaves and stalks, should be cultivated in drills, wide enough apart to admit of cultivation and

full development. If sown broadcast, the fodder is poor, watery
and nearly worthless. Corn fodder contains an excess of carbohydrates for a well-balanced food, and when fed either green or
dry, should be mixed with clover, bran or other nitrogenous food
material. It is eaten with a better relish if cut up, crushed,
moistened, and mixed with bran, oil-meal or cotton-seed meal.

STRAW of any grain is like corn stalks, too rich in carbonaceous
elements to make a perfect food. It lacks flesh-forming materials,
and it is of little value alone as food for working horses. Oats are
often fed in the bundle unthreshed, and are readily eaten by horses.
This practice saves the expense of threshing, and renders the straw
available as food. For horses doing little or no work in winter, such
food will do well as a part of the daily ration. But the unthreshed
bundle should be run through the feed cutter and cut fine. If it is
then dampened and a few quarts of bran, or a pound of linseed or
cotton-seed meal mixed with it, the ratio will be better adapted to
the horse than if fed alone. The greatest drawback to the practice
of keeping the oats unthreshed in the barn until fit to feed, is that
they attract rats and mice.

OATS are pre-eminently the grain for horses, if only one kind
of grain is fed. They not only contain a large per cent of nutrients in
almost the correct ratio for the horse's requirements, but also a peculiar alkaloid, which is gently stimulating. The fibrous husk in which
the grain is enclosed serves a valuable purpose in dividing the mass
in the horse's stomach, and exposing it to the action of the digestive
fluids. Oats should be at least three months old before they are fed.
When new they are difficult to digest, and liable to give a horse the
colic. They should be plump and of full weight. The husk on light
inferior oats is as heavy as on those which are sound and heavy, the
deficiency in weight coming wholly out of the grain. Thirty-two
pounds constitute a legal bushel, but good samples weigh more, running as high as forty-four pounds to the measured bushel. Six quarts
of the latter weigh nearly as much as a peck of the former, and contain far more nutriment. This fact should be taken into consideration in buying and feeding. If fed whole, even to young horses with
good teeth, oats are more or less imperfectly masticated and a part
passes through undigested. Many judicious feeders have them
crushed, to secure more complete mastication.

INDIAN CORN is the great food grain of America, and of the
immense annual crops, aggregating in some years nearly two bil-
lion bushels, the greater part is fed to domestic animals. Corn is

largely used as an article of horse food, either unground or in the form of meal. Corn is a highly concentrated food, heating and deficient in muscle-forming elements. When fed to horses, it should therefore be combined with nitrogenous foods in such proportions as are best adapted to the season, amount of work required, and other conditions. It is quite a usual practice with many horse owners to feed their horses corn in the ear, under the idea of saving the expense of grinding. But this is very questionable economy, for a considerable part of the grain must go through undigested. On the other hand if fed in the form of fine meal, it should be mixed with several times its own bulk of cut hay or other coarse feed to separate the particles and expose them to the action of the digestive fluids of the stomach. If fed alone, corn meal becomes impacted in the stomach, forming a plastic adhesive mass nearly impenetrable to the gastric juice. Severe and in some cases fatal colic is the frequent result. Even if the meal is mixed with ground oats, the mass is too dense to form a safe and desirable food, unless fed in combination with coarser material. Prof. Stewart in his work on "Feeding Animals," says : " We have known of the death of at least a dozen horses, which on examination proved to be caused by feeding corn meal alone. Some feed wet and others dry, because the wet meal may be swallowed with very little mastication, while the dry meal must be masticated until the saliva saturates it, before it can be swallowed ; and the saliva assists digestion. It is, therefore, in better condition for digestion when fed dry than wet. Four of those who had lost horses by feeding meal alone, when they changed the system and fed the meal upon cut hay, first moistened so that the meal adhered to it, and both must be eaten together, had no further losses or even illness of their horses. In our experience of about thirty years in feeding work horses, no ill effects have arisen from feeding corn meal, ground as fine as burr millstones can properly do it, when mixed with cut hay or straw. We have fed horses, from four years old to twenty, upon various concentrated grains, ground into fine meal, and they were always in good health, when the rule of mixing fine meal with cut hay was strictly adhered to."

BARLEY is the principal grain food of horses in many parts of the world. The Arabs feed their famous horses largely on barley ; the French in Algeria have adopted the same practice. In some of the great breeding stables of Illinois barley and oats ground together in proportions varying with the season, are fed to the stallions and mares. The introduction of a black hulless barley into cultivation is likely to lead to still more extensive use of this grain as food for horses. The black hulless variety is not used for malting; it yields large crops in many parts of the Northwest, beyond the "corn belt," and is as easily raised as oats. This new variety seems likely to become an important item in the general grain crops of the country. Barley contains a larger proportion of the elements which produce heat and fat than any other grain, except Indian corn. Moreover, it weighs one half more per bushel than oats, and the hulless variety is still heavier. When either barley or corn and oats are ground and fed together, they should be mixed according to weight, not bulk.

WHEAT BRAN is a valuable article for horse feed, both for its peculiar action on the digestive organs, and as a balance to richer foods. When fed alone, it is generally in the form of warm mash. To make this take four quarts of pure wheat bran, add two teaspoonfuls of salt, pour over it boiling water, and stir quickly till all is wet, but not too thin, cover closely to confine the steam, let it stand until cool and give in the place of the regular feed. Such a mash once a week, while the horse is kept stabled, will gently open the bowels, and promote digestion. It should be given at night, and preferably just before a day of rest, as the immediate effect is somewhat weakening. Bran may also be mixed with ground oats, corn or barley. On this point Prof. Henry, of the University of Wisconsin, writes as follows :

" As a rule we do not give enough importance to the necessity of *variety* in our feed stuffs. If the farmer has oats in abundance, along with hay, he is well satisfied to feed oats and hay to his horses throughout the whole year—perfectly satisfied that they are the best combination possible for the horse. Without doubt clean, bright oats and hay free from dust are the best articles that can be named, but the horse will crave other articles, nevertheless, after he has been fed on these for some time. It is certainly possible where oats have been the only grain feed, to substitute bran for a portion of the oats and maintain the animals perfectly well with the mixed-grain ration. The mills find bran so bulky that they cannot store it successfully in any quantity during the summer and are forced to drop their prices ; as soon as winter comes on they force it up to all the market will bear. Farmers are finding out that bran that can be stored during the summer months without moulding if put in a perfectly dry place where a reasonable circulation of air can be had around it. Such farmers buy while the bran is cheap and make a saving of nearly 50 per cent in the cost compared with winter prices. Of course if everybody goes to buying in the summer, prices will go up, but we may expect bran to maintain lower prices during the summer months."

LINSEED CAKE is largely employed as animal food in England, the greater part of that made in this country being exported there. But Americans are learning its value, and are feeding more of it than formerly. It acts both as a medicine and as a food. It is mildly laxative to the bowels, soothing to the air-passages, and gives gloss to the coat. The "new process" meal contains much less oil than that made by the old process, and is therefore less relaxing and fattening, while the proportion of albuminoids is greater. To make a gruel, the oil-meal is simmered in water until it becomes a mucilagenous mass, into which bran is stirred and the whole fed warm. As a feed substance oil meal is useful mainly to mix in small quantities with other materials. A ration containing six parts of oats, four of corn, and two of linseed meal, would be very nearly equivalent to the oats and beans which form the grain staple of food given to horses in England.

COTTON SEED MEAL is similar in its chemical composition to linseed meal, but is more highly concentrated, and contains a larger proportion of nitrogenous elements. It should be fed with great caution, in small quantities, and never alone.

CARROTS have a food value greater than their composition would indicate. Eighty-five per cent of their bulk is water, and of the solids which remain, nearly one-tenth is fiber. Yet they serve to cool the system, and assist in the digestion of other food. They should be fed a few at a time, two or three times a week. Parsnips have nearly the same composition as carrots, except that they contain even a larger per cent of water. In England and France they are fed in the same way as carrots.

In making up a feeding ration for a horse, the first point is to find out how much the horse will eat ; the next is to regulate the ration according to the weather, and the amount and character of the work the horse is expected to perform. The harder the work and the colder the weather, the greater the proportion of carbohydrates required in the food. The experience of street-car companies, and other corporations which work large numbers of horses, shows that a nutritive ratio of one to six is best for horses kept at hard work in cold weather. In the stables of the West Division Street Railroad of Chicago, where several thousand horses are kept, the food consists mainly of ground oats and corn, with cut hay. The latter is wet sufficiently to make the meal adhere to it, and the whole is mixed together. In warm weather the ground feed consists of two parts of oats and one of corn; in winter there is an equal proportion of each. The great advantages which arise from the practice of grinding the grain and feeding it intimately mixed with cut hay or straw, are that it diminishes waste, promotes more thorough mastication, and the food enters the stomach in the best condition for the action of digestive fluids. Where large numbers of horses are kept at exacting work, there is also economy in grinding the grain food, and cutting the coarser forage. Mill-stones and feed-cutters are cheaper means of crushing and cutting the grain and hay than the muscular power of the horses' jaws, and the use of them gives the horse more time for rest.

A correct idea of the composition of foods is important to every horse-keeper, whether he has one or many, and it is therefore treated here at some length. But it is expected that judgment will be exercised in applying these facts, according to various circumstances. The care and labor required in selecting, cutting and grinding the food for large stables, or for horses from which heavy and constant labor is required, are not always economical where only a family horse is kept. The suburban or village resident can nearly always buy hay and oats of good quality, as well as bran and such roots and other feeding stuffs as are required for wholesome variety. The late Henry William Herbert gave the following general directions, which are well adapted for the daily feeding of a horse weighing from 950 to 1,100 pounds, where oats and uncut hay are the staple articles of food :

" For a gentleman's carriage-horse or roadster, at ordinary work, in its own stable, eight pounds, and from that up to ten, of the very best, richest and most succulent hay is amply sufficient, with twelve quarts of good heavy oats, as a daily allowance. It should be fed with a lock of hay and half a pail of water, the first thing in the morning, on opening the stable ; and when the stable has been aired, cleaned, and littered, should have, after being thoroughly groomed, the other half-pail of water, and—if not going out—four quarts of oats; and when it has eaten these it may have about four or five pounds of hay and be left quiet. If going out early, it should have six quarts of oats at the morning feed, and no hay. If it is standing in the stable, and not to be put to work until afternoon, it should be again watered, and have four quarts more at noon ; and when it returns at night, should be cleaned, watered, fed with oats, and have

(33–34)

FRENCH COACH-HORSE FRANC TIREUR.

the remainder of the hay at night. This will be found amply sufficient to keep the horse in good working condition, when no extraordinary labor—that is to say, not to exceed from ten to twenty miles per diem—is expected of him, and neither extraordinary turns of speed nor feats of endurance. Half a bushel of nicely-washed carrots, given, a few at a time, every week, will be found to improve the coat, to be particularly beneficial to the stomach and wind, and to be very grateful to the animal ; and, in weather and in places where they can be easily provided, a few handfuls of clover, fine meadow grass, or corn stalks and leaves, will cool the blood, give a kindly alterative to the system, keep the bowels moderately open, and please the appetite of the animal. They should not, however, be given too freely, when the horse is at hard work, as they will, perhaps, produce laxity and scouring."

Mr. Lyman F. Abbott, of Maine, gives the following as the result of long practical experience :

"How much will a horse of 1,000 pounds weight require for a daily ration of hay and grain? We give our experience in feeding a family horse which has been kept in stable now for eight years, not having been turned to grass over an hour at a time during the whole period, and in the past five years has not been at grass at all. This horse will weigh some 975 pounds, and has been fifteen years old for a number of years ; is harnessed daily, and but few days in the year pass without its being driven five miles, and frequently two or three times that distance. The past winter its measured and weighed rations have been as follows : Morning, at six o'clock, one quart of cracked corn, half-pound new process linseed meal, one quart bran, good English hay, four pounds. Noon, one quart of cracked corn, and one quart of bran. Night ration same as morning, at same hour. For summer feed, oats are substituted for the main part of the corn, and the night ration of linseed meal discontinued, and one quart of bran, or one pint of middlings added. This feed keeps the animal in fine condition and good spirits. A young horse would probably keep in as good condition with one-third less hay, with the same grain. But the horse which works upon the farm, may be kept economically and in good condition on a different combination of foods.

"If we use corn as the larger portion of the grain food, early cut clover hay is a good fodder to feed with it, as clover is more nitrogenous than corn, and forms a good combination. Corn, on a basis of 75 cents per hundred pounds, and clover hay at 60 cents per hundred pounds, with oats at 45 cents a bushel, would combine a ration as follows : For a horse weighing a thousand pounds, six pounds of corn and six pounds of oats ground together, with twelve pounds of clover hay, would make a good average daily ration. The clover should be run through a cutter and moistened, and the meal incorporated with it. Clean, bright oat straw substituted for half the clover or other hay, and two pounds of linseed meal added, would make a good feed for a work horse, and not add to the cost as figured above.

"For a driving horse nothing can excel oats as a grain food, and for a horse either driving or working, the grain food should exceed in weight the hay or bulky portion of his rations, for the obvious reason that the horse's stomach is small in comparison to the size of the body, and designed to digest concentrated, nutritious food. Every horse-owner should keep on hand linseed meal, or a quantity of flaxseed, and feed it to the animal three or four times a week, or whenever the animal shows signs of constipation. This has a large percentage of muscle-forming material, has a soothing effect upon the stomach, and improves digestion and health."

Overfeeding should be as carefully avoided as underfeeding. Indeed, the consequences of cramming with too rich or too much food are more speedy, and often more fatal, than are those of neglect or insufficiency. A horse standing idle does not require and cannot consume as much food as when it is kept at work. The food necessary to sustain steady labor becomes injurious if continued during a lengthened cessation from work. Its rations must be reduced when it is detained in the stable for any considerable time by bad weather or other cause. Overfeeding and lack of exercise are the source of many serious diseases, the most usual taking the form of paralysis and spinal meningitis.

Regularity in feeding is of great importance. The horse is a good timekeeper as to its own meals, and is worried by any delay or irregularity. Not only should feeding time be strictly observed, but no sudden or violent changes should be made in the character of the food. There is no more prolific cause of colic than a change from an accustomed food to one widely dissimilar, however harmless or suitable it may be when the transition from one to the other is gradual.

Nostrums like nitre, rosin, sulphur and all the so-called " condition powders," should be kept away from a horse, unless used intelligently as medicine for some well-defined ailment. The practice of giving such things regularly or frequently with the feed is pernicious. Saltpetre and rosin are active diuretics, irritating to the kidneys, and their indiscriminate use often leads to serious derangement of those organs.

Salt is doubtless wholesome and beneficial for horses, notwithstanding the contrary opinion of some people who have given attention to the matter. But horses are fond of salt, and thrive better with it than if deprived of it. The best method of supplying this article is to keep a lump of rock salt at all times where the horse can lick it. Receptacles are made of wire for this purpose; but a small wooden or iron box, fastened near the manger or rack, will serve nearly as well.

WATERING.

The horse in a state of nature feeds upon juicy, succulent herbage, and drinks at pleasure from pure water. When these conditions are changed for confinement in the stable or work on the dusty road, with a diet consisting mainly, if not exclusively, of dry hay and grain, the health and well-being of the horse, as well as common humanity, demand careful and judicious attention to the matter of water supply. The water must always be pure and fresh. No animal is more delicate and fastidious about its drink than a horse, and one of them will suffer agonies from thirst rather than quench it with impure, tepid or stale water. It should be given in small quantities and frequently, and never in large draughts, when the horse comes in heated, or immediately before being put to work. Many writers recommend such an arrangement of the water supply as shall keep it constantly within reach of the horse. If the drinking vessel could be kept perfectly clean and free from slime and dirt, with a stream of pure water constantly running in by one pipe while the surplus escapes by another, this kind of an arrangement would be admirable for a horse while it was kept in the stable. But even then it would be necessary to shut off the supply when the horse comes in heated from work. On the whole, probably the common practice of carrying the water to the horse in a bucket, or leading the animal to a trough, is the best practicable. Some horses require more water than others, the quantity varying with the amount of hay it will eat, its propensity to sweat, etc. The water should not be excessively cold. Copious draughts of cold water, when the horse is heated, produce colic, or founder is likely to ensue. If pumped from a cold well it may stand until the chill is taken off. Hard water is much decried as causing harshness in the coat, and soft water is doubtless better. Yet no part of the country produces finer horses than the limestone States of Vermont and

Kentucky If a change is made from soft to hard water, it should be done gradually, as the horse becomes accustomed to it. Where rain water is given it should be kept clean and aerated. Stale, foul water from a neglected cistern is unfit for a horse, and will be refused except in case of extreme thirst.

Horses, when working in the fields, are subjected to great suffering from thirst. From morning till noon, and again from noon till the hour of quitting for the night, the horses are kept in the dusty field, often under a burning sun, without drink. The driver makes frequent visits to the water jug in the shade, without giving a thought to his thirsty horses. If there is no brook or other water supply within convenient distance, a keg of it, with a pail, may be carried along and kept in the shade.

When a horse comes in heated and tired from hard driving, nothing is more grateful and soothing than a few quarts of gruel made by throwing a handful of oatmeal or linseed meal in a gallon of boiling water, letting it steep an hour and then adding a gallon of cold water. If none of this is prepared, a handful of oatmeal in half a bucket of cold water may be given.

CHAPTER III.

BARNS AND STABLES.

In most instances where a horse is kept for family use, it is stabled upon the premises of its owner. The exceptions to this are found in cities. The resident of a large city who keeps one horse is generally obliged to hire it boarded. Its stabling, care and feeding are entrusted to the proprietor of the boarding stable, and the horse is seldom seen by its owner save in harness or under saddle. Such horses are usually in very good hands. However much foundation there may be for Mayhew's vivid pictures of the brutality and trickery of English stablemen, the boarding stables in large American cities are generally in the hands of competent men, who keep a strict eye to business, and whose interest it is that the horses committed to their keeping shall be well fed and cared for. Horses are gregarious in their nature, and other things being equal, one of them enjoys life quite as well in a stable with others as when kept in solitary confinement, unless the absence of stable companions is made up by increased attention and petting from its owner and other members of the household.

But the village or suburban dweller must provide a stable on his own premises. Its style and finish will be governed mainly by the taste and pecuniary ability of the owner. But however plain or elaborate it may be, there are certain essential points. The stable must be cool and airy in summer, warm in winter, thoroughly well ventilated, lighted and drained at all times. It should have a stall, or what is far better, a loose box for the horse, a place for at least one vehicle, a snug mouse-proof harness-closet, and storage for grain and fodder. A cupboard for medicines and small articles is very convenient. It is always desirable to have an extra stall for contingencies. Under no circumstances should a horse be stabled in a basement wholly or partially under ground. Such a stable cannot be made cheerful or wholesome, and a horse kept there suffers in health and spirits. Inveterate cases of scratches, defective vision, impaired digestion, and other evils, are the result. Nor can a horse do well in a dark stable. The change from the wild freedom a horse enjoys in a state of nature, to the drudgery and confinement entailed on it by domestication, is enough without imprisonment in a dark dungeon ; dark stables are prolific sources of blindness.

A stable should be as well lighted as a dwelling house of the same size. The windows may be hung as shown in figure 27, which represents a combined window and ventilator for a stable. The sides are of pine lumber, twenty-six inches long, and one foot wide at the broad end, tapering to one inch wide at the other end. The wider ends are cut to a segment, as shown in the engraving. Quarter-inch holes are bored in the edge of one of these boards. A sash, eighteen by twenty-six inches, with four lights of glass, is screwed to the front edges of the boards. The whole is then hung in place by a pair of wrought iron butts, screwed to the lower side of the sash and to a board firmly nailed upon the inside of the stable, in the rear of the stall. A flat piece of iron, with a quarter-inch hole, or a

Fig. 27.—A SERVICEABLE VENTILATOR.

stout screw-eye is fastened into the stable wall directly over one of the side-boards. Through this an iron pin, *a*, is thrust into a hole in the edge of the side board, to hold the ventilator at any desired angle. When open, as shown in the engraving, a current of air is admitted in the direction indicated by the curved arrow, ventilating the stable without exposing the horse to a direct draught.

While it is objectionable to keep a horse in a dark stable, neither should the light be admitted directly in front, but from one side. Even from the rear is better than from the front. But let us have a light stable, and one where the sun will shine in a part of the day. Light, and above all, the genial rays of the sun, exercise a very important influence upon animal as well as vegetable life. Provide the windows with shutters or blinds, to exclude light when desired, and with facilities for opening. In summer the windows may be replaced with fine wire gauze to exclude the flies.

Perfect drainage is a matter of prime importance. Dampness is a fatal defect in a stable, and is usually the principal cause of unwholesomeness in basements. If the soil upon which the barn stands is naturally damp, it must be drained by porous tiles, laid from two to three feet underground. For draining the stalls no plan is cheaper or more effective than a gutter in the rear of the stalls, leading through the side of the barn to the manure pit, or to the sewer in cities where the liquid manure is of no practical value. Complicated systems of blind drains, with grated openings inside the stable, are almost certain to give forth foul emanations of so-called sewergas, about as bad as no drainage at all.

The foundation of a good horse is its feet. No matter how symmetrical the head and body may be, without sound legs and feet it is next to valueless. The first care, then, for the horse passing a part of every twenty-four hours in its stall, should be for the feet and legs. Standing upon a hard floor is liable to injure the feet. A floor of clay and coal-ashes is desirable for a horse whose feet are liable to become inordinately dry from lack of natural moisture and subject to contraction of the heels. Such a floor should be four or five inches thick, one-third sifted coal-ashes and the remainder moist clay. Make a thin mortar of the clay and add the ashes, working the mass with a hoe, as mortar is made for plastering purposes, until the two are thoroughly incorporated together. When the mortar becomes quite "stiff," put it in place and beat down hard with a rammer of wood, similar to that used by pavers. When dry, this earthen floor will be hard, but it may be moistened where the horse's forward feet come—the hind feet, for obvious reasons, are not subject to the same conditions as regards moisture. Such a floor will become worn by constant use where the most tread comes, but is easily renewed by cutting out portions down through its thickness and replenishing with new material. A horse predisposed to tender feet, and liable to contraction of heels, with other feet and ankle troubles, if obliged to occupy his stall half of the time or more, will do better upon the earthen floor.

A great deal has been written about stable floors, and elaborate directions given for constructing them of stone, concrete, asphaltum, and cemented brick. But there are objections to all of these materials, so serious that none of them has ever found general favor in this country. Stone is hard and cold for the horse ; concrete and asphaltum break up under the tramping of the iron-shod feet; brick is liable to the same objection, and the additional one of absorbing the offensive fluids, and a dirt floor very soon becomes a quagmire. The material almost universally employed in this country is sound pine or spruce planks, properly laid. The floor should be double, the lower planks lying transversely of the stall, and the upper ones, two inches thick, are laid lengthwise, and only as long as the stall itself. There must be a slight slope to the rear for drainage, but this should never exceed one inch in six feet. If any greater, it compels the horse to stand in an unnatural position, with a constant strain upon the tendons of the legs. It is no wonder that a horse standing on a rapidly sloping floor, seeks temporary relief by turning crosswise of the stall. A thin coat of melted pitch or coal tar upon the lower course of planks, before the upper course is laid, will protect it from moisture and decay. If the entire floor is given repeated coats of crude petroleum, until thoroughly satura-

Fig. 28.—HAY-RACK AND FEED-TROUGH.

ted, it will not only act as a preservative, but also prevent to a large extent the absorption of offensive liquids. A horse-stall should be five-a-half feet wide in the clear, and six is better, and there should be at least fifteen feet of space from the head of the stall to the wall in the rear, to allow for backing out the horse.

There should never be less than eight feet of clear space above the floor, and ten feet is much better. If hay or other forage is kept in the loft, the upper floor should be matched and lined or otherwise made perfectly tight, to keep out the breath and odors of the stable. A shute, extending from the manger to the roof, with doors on one or more sides, may be made to serve the double purpose of ventilating the stable, and passing down hay and straw. It should be made flaring towards the bottom to allow free passage of hay. A slatted ventilator is built directly over it on the roof; and a valve at the lower extremity may be wholly or partially closed, whenever the inclemency of the weather requires it.

There are many forms of hay-racks and feed-troughs. Several styles of iron fixtures are convenient and durable. But the worst form is the old fashioned overhead hay-rack. It is wholly inconsistent with the habits and structure of the horse, which in a state of nature does not, like a giraffe, take its food from trees, but from the ground. Besides the unnatural strain caused by reaching up to a high rack, the dust hay seed and chaff are drawn into the throat, lungs and eyes of the horse. The rack shown in figure 28 is cheaply built, and free from all the objections to a high rack. The vertical slats are four feet long, of any tough hard wood. Saplings with the bark on are as good as anything. The ends, tapered off to the proper size,

Fig. 29.—PERSPECTIVE VIEW OF SMALL BARN.

are set into holes bored in scantlings. The lower side of the rack is sixteen inches above the floor. The opposite side is boarded up as shown. The bottom of the rack is of slats, two inches apart, to allow the escape of dust and seeds. Resting on the floor below the rack is a trough for oats or other feed. This is ten inches deep, and of any desired width and length. It is drawn out to be filled, and then pushed back within reach of the horse. Instead of this a permanent feed-box may be made at one end of the rack, a few slats being left out for the purpose. The hay-shute opens directly into the rack.

The perspective view and plan shown in figures 29 and 30 are of a very cheap and plain barn of the simplest style. The upright part is fourteen feet wide by sixteen long, with sixteen-foot posts. The lean-to is ten feet wide, sixteen long, and eight feet high at the eaves. The sills all around rest upon piers of field stone, or in their absence, on cedar blocks set below the frost line. The first floor, figure 30, has a carriage floor with a flight of stairs to the hay-loft. Beneath the stairs is a closet for harness. The lean-to has a box-stall ten by twelve feet, with a passage giving access to the oat-bin and hay-rack. The barn is enclosed in vertical boarding, with three-inch battens. The roof is shingled. A barn of this size and style can be built in good substantial manner for three hundred dollars.

There are many advantages in the octagon form for a barn, as will be seen by the accompanying illustrations, showing a barn which, like the preceding one, is of dimensions to admit of its being placed upon a lot only twenty-five feet wide. Figure 31 gives a perspective view; figure 32 shows the floor plan, and figure 33 one-half the roof plan. The barn is twenty-four feet in diameter from side to side, each one of the eight sides being ten feet wide. The posts are sixteen feet high; the first floor nine feet in the clear; the loft six

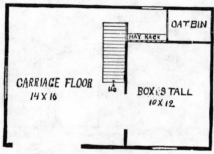

Fig. 30.—GROUND PLAN OF BARN.

feet to top of plates, and twenty feet to the apex of the roof. A hay door directly over the main entrance to the barn affords means for filling the loft. The first floor is divided through the center by a partition, upon one side of which are a box stall, nine by twelve feet, an open stall five and a half feet wide, and a passage way. The other half is occupied by a carriage floor eighteen feet long, at one end of which is the harness closet, and at the other a flight of stairs leading to the loft. Opening out of the harness closet is a granary, and a capacious bin for oats or other feed is under the stairs. The box stall is entered by a sliding door from the open stall, and also by a swing-door from the carriage floor. The latter door is divided horizontally a little above the middle, so that the upper part may be left open, when desired, for ventilation. The lower part is fastened, when closed, with a latch, the upper portion by a bolt, and the two may be firmly coupled by two hooks and staples. In the rear

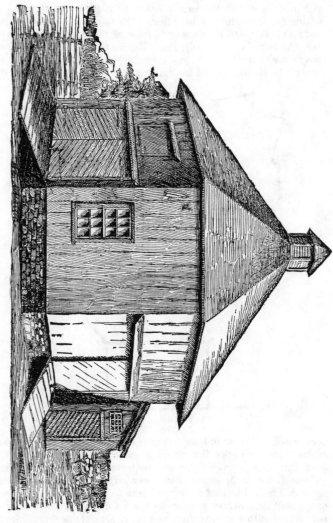

Fig. 31.—PERSPECTIVE VIEW OF OCTAGON BARN.

of the stall is a window, protected on the inside by a wire netting with inch meshes. In warm weather both are replaced by a wire netting fine enough to exclude flies. The hay is supplied through a shute extending to within a few inches of the ventilator above the roof. This tapers gradually from bottom to top, so that hay will pass freely through it. A door in one side of it, two feet above the floor of the loft, is opened to admit the hay, and a valve above this

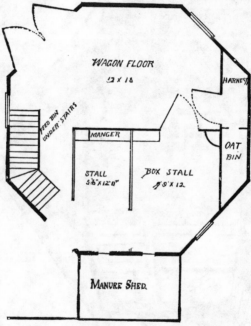

WAGON FLOOR
12 X 18

HARNESS

FEED BIN UNDER STAIRS

MANGER

OAT BIN

STALL
5 6"X 12 0"

BOX STALL
9 9 X 12

MANURE SHED.

Fig. 32.—GROUND PLAN.

door, working like an ordinary damper in a stove-pipe, affords means of checking ventilation through it in extremely cold weather. The shute thus acts as a ventilator, and protects the hay from all breath, gases and odors of the stable. Four feet above the stable floor it terminates in a rack, like that shown in figure 28. In the opposite corner of the stall is an iron or wooden feed-box for grain. The open stall is provided with a similar shute and rack. The stable door slides on a track protected from rain and snow. The two large doors are hung by stout hinges. The barn is boarded up with two thicknesses of vertical siding, with building paper between, the joints covered by battens, and the roof is shingled.

Nearly all the timbers for such a barn are short. Eight sills, six by eight inches, ten feet long, are morticed and pinned together at the angles, and a sill of the same width and thickness, twenty-four feet long, extends through the center. At each angle of the frame is a vertical post, four by six inches, sixteen feet long notched on the outer face to receive three courses of girders at proper intervals, upon which the siding is nailed. The floor beams are two by eight inches, and laid sixteen inches apart from centers. The roof is "half-pitch," that is, the apex is twelve feet higher than the

Fig. 33.—ONE HALF OF ROOF FRAME.

top of the plates. The apex, however, is truncated by the octagon frame of the ventilator, three feet in diameter, as shown in figure 33, and rafters two by six inches, sixteen feet and a half long, extend from each angle of the plates to the ventilator frame. Midway between every two of these is a rafter, fifteen and a half feet long, from the center of each plate. On each side of this, at equal intervals and parallel with it, are two rafters two by four inches, one twelve and the other seven feet long. The foot of each rests upon the plate, and the summit is spiked or bolted to the side of the longest rafter. This leaves the spaces between the rafters very nearly uniform, and the four short ones support the longest. At each inner angle of the plates is a block four by four inches, fourteen inches long, beveled to fit the angle, and secured in place by half-inch bolts, the heads of which are countersunk in the outer face of the plates to be out of way of the siding. These secure the plates from spreading. The entire roof is thus a single truss, needing no support from the inside. The manure shed is on the side

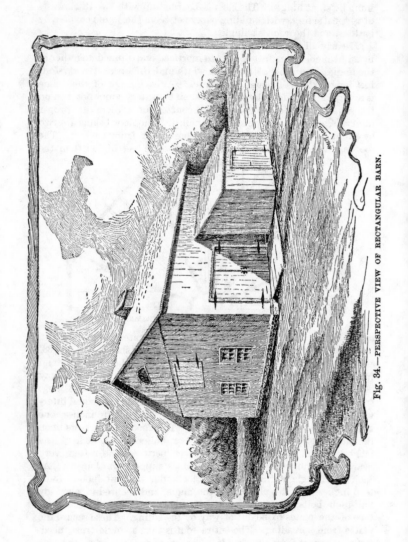

Fig. 34.—PERSPECTIVE VIEW OF RECTANGULAR BARN.

next to the stalls. As will be seen, the stalls are doubly protected from direct exposure to cold air on nearly every side, yet they are provided with abundant light and ventilation.

Figure 34 gives a perspective and figure 35 the plan, of a rectangular barn occupying about the same space as the octagon last described. It is twenty-five by twenty feet, with posts sixteen feet. Two swing doors, each four feet wide, give access to the carriage

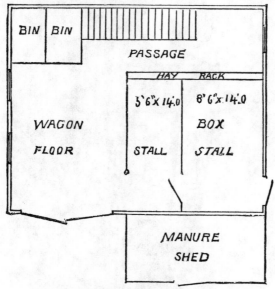

Fig. 35.—GROUND PLAN.

floor. At the right of this are an open stall and a box-stall. In the rear of the carriage-floor is a granary with separate bins for oats and other feed. A passage-way, six feet wide, extends along the front of the stalls, and gives access to the mangers and feed boxes. The box-stall is reached by an outer door, and also communicates with the open stall by a door divided horizontally a little above the middle. The upper part of the latter door may be opened for ventilation. A manure shed, eight by fourteen feet, is attached to the barn in the rear of the stalls. The sides of the barn are covered with vertical boarding and battens; the roof shingled. It is a very simple and cheaply-built form.

Fig. 36.—PERSPECTIVE VIEW OF BARN AND SHED.

For more extensive premises than a single village lot, it is sometimes considered desirable to have an open shed and yard adjoining the barn. Figure 36 shows a barn and shed, designed by Mrs. M. L. Knowles, of Orchard Hill Stock Farm, Michigan. The barn is eighteen by thirty-nine feet. On the ground floor, figure 37, are a box-stall twelve feet square, and an open stall six by twelve feet. In the rear of these stalls is the floor for grooming and harnessing, with harness-closet and stairway, beneath the latter of which are bins for grain. A door at the foot of the stairs opens into the ma-

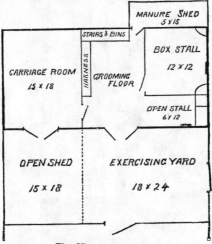

Fig. 37.—GROUND PLAN.

nure shed, from which there is an outer door into the garden. Double doors open from the main floor into the yard. Beyond the floor is the carriage room, away from the stalls, where no fumes of ammonia can reach the vehicles to corrode the leather-work, and fill the upholstery with stable odors. Wide double doors open from this floor into an open shed, which extends entirely across one end of the yard. The box-stall is provided with a hay shute in one corner, and a feed box in the other. The door is divided horizontally in the middle, and each half provided with hangings and fastenings, so that the upper half can be left open, when desired, for ventilation. The open stall is of ample width to allow a horse to lie down in it, and is also provided with a feed box and a manger, to which the hay is supplied by means of a shute from the loft. The open

Fig. 38.—PERSPECTIVE VIEW OF HORSE AND CARRIAGE BARN.

shed is not designed as a receptacle of broken-down wheel-barrows, wrecked wagons, garden rubbish, or a roost for poultry, but is to be kept in good order for the horse to run under, when the weather is too inclement for long exposure in the yard.

The accompanying illustrations show a barn elegant in appearance, convenient and useful. As will be seen by the perspective view, figure 38, it has a hip roof with gables on the front and each end, and is surmounted by a cupola. The main structure is forty-four feet long by thirty wide, with sixteen-foot posts ; the "annex" is sixteen feet by thirty, making a total frontage of sixty feet. The main part stands upon stone piers which raise the floor two feet above the ground. The floor of the carriage and tool house is flat on

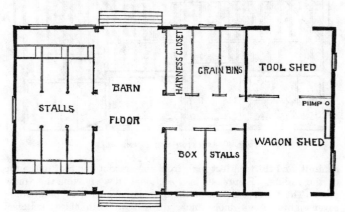

Fig. 39.—GROUND PLAN.

the ground, and may be paved or constructed of concrete, asphaltum, or coal-tar and gravel. Figure 39 shows the ground plan. A driveway fourteen feet wide extends entirely across the middle of the main part, with six open stalls on one side, and on the other are two box stalls, a harness closet, and bins for oats and feed. A large window in the end and two smaller ones on each side furnish ample light and ventilation for the stalls. All these windows may be removed in summer and the openings covered with gauze to exclude flies. Feed passages are provided at the heads of the open stalls, which give access to the mangers and racks. The doors are each five feet wide and ten feet high. A passageway six feet wide extends through the entire length of the barn, with an inclined platform down to the wagon room. This room is furnished with a pump and watering trough. The water supply may be provided by a well or preferably a cement-lined cistern, to which is conducted the water from the roof.

The first story is ten feet high in the clear. The hight from the upper floor to the apex of the roof is eighteen feet, making, with the gables, a large amount of storage room for hay or other forage. The cupola is eight feet square at the base, tapering to four feet at the

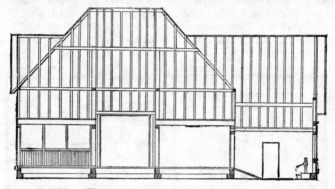

Fig. 40.—SECTION AND FRAME PLAN.

summit, and thirteen feet high from the apex of the roof to the top of the railing. Figure 40 is a sectional view showing the frame plan. The lower ten feet of the barn is covered with pine siding seven-eights of an inch thick, dressed on both sides, matched and rabbeted, above that is vertical siding dressed and matched. The roof and cupola are shingled. The estimated cost, with first-class work inside and out, is $990. A barn could be built on the same general style and ground plan, without the cupola, covered with vertical siding and battened, for about $500.

CHAPTER IV.

STABLE MANAGEMENT.

THE stable may be made a wholesome, pleasant home for the horse, or a wretched dungeon. Even when it is expensively built, and the food unobjectionable in quality and quantity, if there is a lack of proper daily care and attention, the animal will suffer in health and condition. The horse is the most cleanly and intelligent of dumb animals. In a state of nature it lives in the open air, and is free from disease. In the domestic condition a perfectly sound horse is the exception rather than the rule. Any one who has seen a newly captured mustang, prancing and cavorting at the end of its lariat, every muscle quivering with animation, would fail to recognize it in the sorry beast it becomes after a few years of confinement in a stable, with the average treatment it is likely to receive. Mayhew paints the picture in his usual glowing colors as follows :

"Horses, when in a wild state, are gregarious, or congregate in herds. Man captures such a quadruped and places it in a stable, built to enforce the extreme of solitary confinement. The plain is the natural abode of the herd ; on their speed depends both their pleasure and safety. Man ties the domesticated horse to a manger, and pays a groom to enforce absolute stagnation upon innate activity. Before subjugation, the creature fed off the surface of the earth. Man builds a house specially designed for the captive, in which the corn is placed on a level with the chest, and the hay is stationed as high up as the head. The animal is gifted with affections ; it longs to gratify their promptings ; it yearns for something upon which its abundant love may gush forth—a fellow-prisoner—a goat—a dog— a cat—a fowl ; no matter what, so it be some living object on which may be lavished that excess of tenderness which, confined to its own breast, renders being miserable. Man esteems it his primary duty to clear the stable of all possible companionship ; but the creature which would rejoice, were it only permitted to worship its enslaver, he rarely approaches without a loud voice, a harsh word or a harsher blow, announcing his presence to the captive. The inhabitant of such a prison, the domesticated horse, miserably drags through a shortened life, under human *protection*. The nearest approach it can make to freedom is its period of exhausting labor. It always rejoices to quit its confinement ; but enfeebled by imprisonment, and subservient to man's exactions, it ever gladly returns to the place of its sorrow.   It lives in so limited a space that, in comparison with the dimensions of its abode, a man in a sentry-box dwells in a mansion; or a lion in a cage roams over a domain.   A reasonable and intelligent being commands his horse to be fastened to such a spot, and supposes that a living organism is to endure the confinement which does not permit the body to turn round ; that animated functions are to exist where most ordinary exercises are rendered impossible ; nevertheless he anticipates the creature will appear bounding with health in answer to his requirements."

Among the horses in this country kept for family use there is probably more suffering from mistaken kindness and lack of skill and judgment, than from deliberate cruelty or willful neglect.   An immense mass of empiricism, prejudice and false notions in relation to horse management in health and disease has become traditional, and is handed down from one generation to another.   Even when the horse is in apparent health, with no morbid symptoms whatever, it is bled, purged and blistered ; harsh diuretics and "condition powders" of unknown composition are administered, with no very definite or intelligent aim, but under the vague idea that such treatment will somehow improve the condition and appearance of the horse.   If we are to retain the pristine health and vigor of the horse under the artificial conditions of domestic servitude, we must furnish it as far as possible with equally pure air, wholesome food and water it has while running wild.

In the first place, the stable must be kept perfectly clean at all times.   If allowed to remain in such a condition that if a man stays ten minutes his clothing becomes saturated with pungent ammoniacal odors, it is not a fit place in which to keep a horse.   The animal cannot retain perfect health in an atmosphere loaded with foul gases.   The stalls and floor must be cleaned every morning and kept clean.   The droppings and wet, foul litter should not be tossed through a hole behind the stall, and left piled up there in a reeking dunghill, with the gases and odors of fermentation penetrating the stable.   To say nothing of the waste of manure, which is often an item of some importance, such a practice is utterly incompatible with pure air in the stable.   The manure and litter should be kept in a sheltered place and frequently sprinkled with some absorbent, as gypsum, swamp muck, or if nothing better is at hand, dry coal ashes or road dust.   During warm weather the stalls, gutters and entire floor should be washed frequently with plenty of water.   Dry land plaster sprinkled plentifully on the floor will absorb ammoniacal emanations, but when wet it becomes a sticky, objectionable mass. A solution of copperas, at the rate of one ounce to two gallons of water, sprinkled freely in the stable, is a very effective deodorizer. When the stable is cleaned up in the morning the partially soiled bedding which is to be used again should be removed to some other part of the stable to dry, and never thrown under the manger, or near the horse's head, in accordance with a quite too common custom. How would the owner or groom enjoy having such an odorous mass under his own table? For handling bedding the wooden stable fork, figure 41, is more convenient than the steel-tined forks, and involves less risk of accidental injury to the feet and legs of the horse. Every vessel used in giving food and water must be kept

Fig. 41.—GIFFORD'S STABLE FORK.

scrupulously clean. Wooden feed-boxes in which dampened food is given, soon become sour and musty if neglected. Iron ones are better. A decent horse will nearly starve rather than take its food from a sour, ill-smelling receptacle.

Poultry should never be permitted to enter the stable, or any part of the barn. If allowed to roost there, they are likely to spread vermin. They befoul the hay-mow and any carriages to which they have access, rob the horse of its grain, and soil its feed-box. Rats and mice are not so easily excluded, but they can be kept out of grain-bins by nailing strips of tin over all angles and cracks.

VENTILATION AND DRAINAGE.

The family horse is likely to suffer more for lack of pure air than farm horses. The former is usually kept in a small tightly built stable, while the latter are housed in one corner of a roomy barn which, whatever it may lack, is abundantly airy. Greater attention is therefore required to furnish judicious ventilation to the smaller and more carefully built stable of the family horse. It may seem strange that horses which run at large on the ranges of the West the entire year, with no shelter from the bitter cold and driving storms of winter, are remarkably sound in wind, while the petted favorites, kept blanketed in warm stables, are constantly liable to attacks which affect their organs of respiration. Dr. Felix L. Oswald writes concerning this point as follows :

" If the genesis of pulmonary affections were more clearly under-

stood, the supposed cause would in fact be valued as the most effective cure, and that catarrh and influenzas are more frequent in winter than in summer, is due exclusively to the circumstance that stables, as well as houses, are most outrageously stuffy at a time when
cold weather furnishes a pretext for keeping doors and windows
tightly closed. Intensely cold weather may disinfect the in-door atmosphere in spite of such precaution, as in the Arctic regions, where
the frost of the polar nights lowered the temperature of the Esqui-
maux hovels below zero, and where consequently pulmonary diseases,
according to the unanimous testimony of Arctic travelers, are almost entirely unknown. But our latitude enjoys neither the advantages or disadvantages of that arrangement. Our Northwest States
experience polar waves that would make a Greenlander feel quite at
home ; but such snaps alternate with days that would give a Cuban
refugee no cause of complaint, and these warm spells are the har-
vest-times of catarrh seeds. After a week's rain, the sun may glare
out in midwinter and make the air feel positively sultry ; but, according to instructions, the groom of a crowded stable continues to keep
the doors carefully closed ; horses, ' off their feed,' for some cause or
other, are kept in-doors day and night, and some fine morning the
zymotic hot-house proves to have developed its fruit in the form of
malignant catarrh. The hot stench of the foul miasma den has at last
overcome the disease-resisting powers of creatures whose ancestors
roamed the airy highlands of American mountains ; the cells of their
lung-tissue have become clogged with the constant influx of atmospheric impurities, as river-beds would become choked with the deposit of an incessant mud-deluge, and under the combined influence
of heat and moisture the festering accumulations have developed the
germs of morbific organisms. With the aid of pure out-door air, the
self-regulating tendency of the animal system would promptly eject
such intruders ; but that air is now excluded more carefully, however ; the affected animals are kept in their stables ; the resources of
their vitality are still further reduced by bleeding and debilitating
cathartics, and under such exquisite combination of favorable conditions the development of the disease here assumes the phase of a
contagious influenza, or a similar ' unaccountable plague.' "

Many well built stables have rooms for the coachman or groom
in the upper story, with conveniences for warming it. In such
places a ventilating tube from the stable may open into the chimney,
and the current of warm air will create sufficient suction to carry off
all impure air from below.

In warm weather ventilation is still more necessary if possible
than in cold. The windows are taken out and replaced by screens

of wire netting to exclude flies. If the interior doors are made in halves, as described in chapter III, the upper half may be left open. A horse in a box stall greatly enjoys standing at such a door with his head thrust out of the open part, watching with apparent interest all that is passing around him. It is certainly a relief from confinement in a sultry stall.

Perfect drainage must be maintained. If the drains are clogged the air of the stable becomes humid, and the horse shivers in cold weather, and suffers much more from heat in summer. Dampness in a stable is the prolific source of many forms of disease.

BEDDING.

A comfortable bed is as necessary for a horse as for a man. Indeed, of the two, the man would doubtless suffer less if obliged to sleep on a bare floor, than the more bulky horse. The horse's bed should be of sufficient thickness, spread smoothly and evenly, so that there are no heaps, hummocks or hollows. Wheat straw is the most common material for bedding. It is cheap, easily handled, and can be made comfortable. The straw of oats and barley is less commonly used, not from any inferiority for this purpose, but because they possess greater feeding value. Sawdust is used to some extent in the vicinity of saw-mills. Forest leaves, gathered in autumn and kept in a dry place, make very good bedding, and add more to the value of manure than any other material used. The pressed peat-moss recently introduced from Germany is superior in many respects to all other substances for stable bedding. It is as soft as feathers, elastic, and possesses many times greater capacity for absorption than straw or saw-dust. It is pressed in bales of convenient size for handling, and a stock sufficient for several months requires very little room for storage. It is in fact sphagnum moss, like that largely used by florists for various purposes. It is found in peat swamps everywhere, and the fact that the imported article only is sold in our markets, arises from the greater cheapness of labor in Germany rather than from lack of the material in this country.

Whatever the material used, the bedding should be cleared up every morning, the droppings and foul litter carried to the manure shed or other suitable receptacle, and the unsoiled portion, together with all that may be dried for further use, put by itself in an empty stall or a shallow box kept for the purpose in a convenient place. At night the bed is to be re-made with the old bedding at the bottom, and fresh material laid smoothly above it.

GROOMING.

A horse which is kept in the stable when it is not at work, requires frequent grooming or currying. "It is to the stabled horse," says Youatt, "highly fed, and little or irregularly worked, that grooming is of the highest consequence. Good rubbing with the brush or the currycomb opens the pores of the skin, circulates the blood to the extremities of the body, produces free and healthy perspiration, and stands in the room of exercise. No horse will carry a fine coat, without either unnatural heat or dressing. They both effect the same purpose, but the first does it at the expense of health and strength; while the second, at the same time that it produces a glow on the skin and a determination of the blood to it, rouses all the energies of the frame. It would be well for the proprietor of the horse if he were to insist, and to see that his orders are really obeyed, that the fine coat in which he and his groom so much delight, is produced by honest rubbing, and not by a heated stable and thick

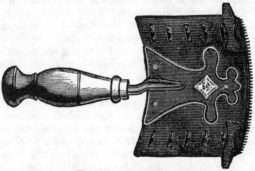

Fig. 42.—CURRYCOMB.

clothing, and, most of all, not by stimulating or injurious spices. The horse should be regularly dressed every day, in addition to the grooming that is necessary after work." To which Henry William Herbert adds: "It is true in a measure, that the necessity of regular dressing, wisping, currying, brushing, and hard rubbing is far greater in the case of highly pampered horses, fed in the most stimulating manner, principally on grain, kept in hot stables, always a little above their work, and ready at all times to jump out of their skins from the exuberance of their animal spirits; yet it is necessary to all housed and stabled horses; and the farmer, no less than the owner of fast trotters, will find his advantage in having his horse curried and washed before feeding in the morning, in the in-

creased play of his spirit, and in the gayety and fitness of the animal for his work; and if, when he brings him in at night, reeking
with sweat, drenched with rain or snow, his thighs and belly plastered with thick mud, and his legs covered, as cart-horses' legs
mostly are, with thick hair, saturated with cold water, and clogged
with particles of mud and sand, he neglects to have him thoroughly
cleaned, and made dry and comfortable for the night, he not only
commits an act of gross cruelty, but wholly disregards his own interest. Unless a horse be cleaned and groomed when in such a condition, he cannot be kept in health ; and if he be fed freely when in
such a state—although the cart-horse is less liable to such ailments
from his hardier habits and less impressive constitution—the chances
are that soon he will be attacked by inflammation of the bowels, or
lungs, or spasmodic colic—the race-horse, fast trotter, or highly bred
and highly fed roadster would be so attacked, to a certainty—and
the failure to dry and cleanse the legs of such a horse, especially if

Fig. 43.—GROOMING BRUSH.

there be a draft of cold wind blowing upon the heels from a crevice
under the stable door, as is generally the case in the common farm
stable, will be almost certainly succeeded by that troublesome,
dangerous and foul disease, known as 'grease,' or more commonly in
America as 'the scratches.'"

The principal implements employed in grooming are the curry-
comb and brush, to which are added a scraper for removing water
or sweat, a whisk broom, a comb and special brush for the mane,
rubbing-cloths, etc. The horse should never be curried in the stall or
box where it eats and stands through the day and sleeps at night.
In fine weather the work is best performed in the open air, at other
times on the floor of the barn, or in a wide stall kept for the purpose. It is something of an art to handle a currycomb with a deft
light touch which will accomplish the object without torturing the
horse. The most common form of comb is shown in figure 42. They
are usually too sharp when first purchased, and should be partially
smoothed by a file, grindstone or by simply rubbing on any gritty
stone. There are many forms of brushes, some of which we illustrate. Figure 43 is a cheap root brush for removing sweat or

dandruff.   There are also more expensive and very effective brushes, with leather backs, which fit themselves to the irregularities of the horse's surface.

Special care must be used in handling the currycomb on the bony parts of the head and face.   When they are properly dressed, the neck, shoulders, body and legs are gone over, the operator holding the comb in one hand and the brush in the other.   With the former the hair is gently and lightly lifted, and the scurf and dandruff loosened, while the latter follows, removing all extraneous matters which have been loosened by the comb.   Then the horse is polished down with wisps of straw and rubbing cloths.   The mane and tail should never be dressed with the currycomb, as it will pull out the hair. Coarse combs are made of hard rubber for this purpose, and

one of them, with a brush of any good pattern, are the proper implements.   In spring when the horse is shedding its winter coat, care should be taken not to remove the old hair too rapidly.   The joints at the hips, hocks and other places where the bones are near the surface should not be touched with the curry-

Fig. 44.—SWEAT SCRAPER.

comb.   The legs demand special care in removing all dirt from the fetlocks and pasterns.   The dressing in all places where the currycomb cannot be used, must be done with the brush, wisps and cloth.

When the horse is brought in drenched with rain or wet with perspiration, the moisture is best removed by means of the scraper. There are various forms of these useful implements, one of which is shown in figure 44.   Others are two-handed, each consisting of a long strip of steel or brass with a handle at each end.   The scraper is passed over the neck and all accessible parts of the body, with a steady gentle pressure, repeated as often as is necessary to remove all excess of water and mud.   If the weather is cold the clothing is put on, and the legs plunged, two at the time, in warm water to soak off the dirt.   For this and many other occasions when it is desirable to bathe the feet and legs, every stable should be provided with a suitable tub.   One may easily be made by sawing an oak barrel in two at the bung, and nailing a board on the head, flush with the ends of the staves, to support the pressure from within.   A few moments bathing will loosen the mud and greatly refresh the horse.   The fore-legs are then rubbed with wisps of straw until thoroughly dry, and the hind ones treated in the same manner. In hot weather it is needful only to scrape and lightly blanket a wet horse, wash the legs off with a sponge or water brush, and rub them dry. It is exceedingly injurious to dash cold water on a horse's legs from a bucket, or squirt it on from a hose. Violent disorders are sometimes induced by such practices. If the horse comes in heated and exhausted from a long or fast drive, special care is required. Shut the doors and keep the horse out of the draft, give it a few swallows of water, scrape off the sweat, throw on a light blanket and rub dry with wisps and a cloth, "rub rag," as horsemen call them, give a little more water, and a little hay, let the horse rest for an hour in a single stall, give the legs a good hand rubbing, groom thoroughly, then lead the horse to its box stall, put on the night clothing, feed and bed down, and leave it for the night. If there is no tub for this purpose, the legs may be washed with a large sponge. In any case, whenever the legs are washed, warm water must always be used, and the legs rubbed dry as rapidly as possible.

If the washing and drying are not thoroughly carried out, it is far better to omit it. A superficial washing which will only clean the ends of the hair, and leave the mud adhering to the skin, can be of little benefit. Still less will it be if the legs are not rubbed wholly dry. The extremities have invariably a weak circulation, they are farthest away from the center of blood supply, and there is in consequence always a tendency to be cold, unless during movement; therefore it is obvious that leaving the hair wet must still further aggravate the matter by chilling the skin, lowering its vitality, and disposing it to disease. Yet the horse must not be allowed to stand all night plastered with mud. If it comes in late, or for any other reason warm water and thorough rubbing dry are unattainable, remove the thickest of the mud with a scraper followed by an old broom, rub the legs thoroughly with hay wisps, wrap them in flannel bandages, and prepare the horse for the night as indicated above. The importance of bandages for horses that are required to perform fast or hard work can hardly be overestimated. Windgalls are very unsightly, and depreciate the value of the animal. Horses at fast work for any length of time invariably have them. Swathing the legs in bandages will not only tend to prevent this, but go a long way to clear up old standing cases. Pressure promotes absorption of the fluid, and by these means cures, while it prevents effusion by supporting the circulation. Racehorses always stand in bandages, and there are no better legs than theirs.

In the stable, as everywhere else, the horse should be treated with unvarying kindness. Harsh, ill-tempered language and treatment are certain to sour the temper, and impair the value of the horse, while kind, pleasant words and gentle treatment will just as surely win its confidence and obedience. No animal is more sensitive to kindness than the horse. A few caressing pats of the hand, an occasional lump of sugar, or apple, with kind words, will go far towards establishing relations between the dumb servant and the master which are greatly to the advantage of both. No one should ever be permitted to tickle or tease the horse, either in the stable or out of it. Whipping a horse while it stands in its stall is an extreme of cruelty and folly, which the animal never forgets.

CLOTHING.

The health, comfort and appearance of the family horse require a certain amount of artificial covering. A horse which is well groomed and cared for has a skin more sensitive than one left exposed to the vicissitudes of the weather. The former, while standing idle in the stable must be kept covered, if the stable is properly ventilated and not too warm. It is essential also for the maintenance of a fine glossy coat. The amount of clothing varies somewhat according to the character of the work required of the horse. Hunters, trotters and running horses require an outfit almost as extensive and varied as the trousseau of a fashionable bride, but the needs of the family horse kept for moderate work are quite limited. Figure 45 shows a horse arrayed in what is called a full walking suit. It consists of a hood which envelopes the head, ears and neck, a breast piece, and a quarter piece which covers the body. The latter is secured in place by a roller or surcingle which is provided with pads, to relieve the spine of undue pressure, and broad enough for comfort to the horse. A girth of narrow plain webbing bearing sharply on the back is a very defective substitute for a good roller. The material and finish of horse clothing vary with the expense. A handsome full suite, including kneecaps, in addition to the articles shown in our engraving, costs from thirty to fifty dollars. A good substantial one, without embroidered ornaments, may be had for fifteen, and a good plain blanket or quarter piece for two to five dollars. Breast pieces cost from fifty cents to five dollars each, according to quality and finish. Hoods are very little used, except on horses used for sporting purposes. The breast piece affords a desirable protection for the region of the heart and lungs. It is useful not only in the stable, but may also be retained when driving in cold, raw weather. Horse clothing for cold weather is usually made of kersey. For summer a light sheet of linen or calico is useful to protect the horse from dust and flies. It is well to have at least one extra blanket for a change, as clothing worn constantly becomes filled with sweat and dirt, requiring occasional cleaning. It is also much better to have one suit for night wear and another for the day. In addition to the close-fitting clothing, a large blanket, which covers the animal from ears to

Fig. 45.—HORSE ARRAYED IN FULL WALKING SUIT.

croup, is very useful to throw over a horse which is brought in wet with rain or sweat. Such blankets are made of woolen fabric, and cost from seven to ten dollars each.

It is never advisable to retain the quarter piece under the harness when driving or working, even if the horse is clipped. It is soon wet with perspiration, and as soon as the motion ceases and the horse stands still, it becomes cold and frozen, causing great discomfort and serious risk. But a blanket should always be carried along to throw over the horse whenever it is stopped. To leave a horse standing unprotected in the wind and cold, is not only a piece of thoughtless cruelty, but it may induce acute and fatal disease.

A horse cover of light rubber cloth, like that shown in figure 46, is very useful when it is necessary to drive in stormy weather. Put on over the harness, it does not heat and sweat a horse like a woolen blanket, but affords greatly needed protection against the pitiless pelting of rain or snow.

STALLS AND LOOSE BOXES.

In every instance, where it is possible to provide a box stall, it should be done. In some of the breeding and racing stables each horse has a loose box not less than twenty feet square. But a box stall nine by twelve feet is a palatial hall in comparison with a single stall, in which it is compelled to stand tied hour after hour. The monotony of the stall is wearisome to an animal of such quick intelligence as the horse. An ox or cow, after it has eaten its food, will stand and chew its cud for hours, the picture of content; but a horse is not a ruminant, and for want of other employment will find some way of passing the dull hours in its stall which is quite likely to end in a permanent bad habit. A great part of this is obviated if the horse is allowed to stand loose in a box stall, where it can turn around freely, roll over and lie down at its ease.

Where a box stall is not to be had, great care must be exercised in tying the horse in a single stall. The halter-strap or rope must be left just long enough to permit the horse to lie down, and no more. If too long, there is great danger that the horse may get one foot over it and thus become cast in the stall. The English method, which is also adopted to some extent in this country, is to let the tie-rein or "collar-rope," as they call it, run loosely through a bolt-ring in the edge of the manger. At the other end of the rope is a weight or sinker of wood loaded with lead, heavy enough to take up all the slack in the tie-rope as the horse moves its head to or from the ring. The rope is long enough to allow the weight to rest upon the floor when the horse's head is close to the manger. The objection to this arrangement is that it maintains a constant and tiresome, even if slight, strain upon the muscles of the head and neck. A good American halter, made adjustable and well-fitted to the head, is more used than the English neck-strap for restraining a horse in its stall. If there is any disposition manifested to pull on the halter, a rope is better and more secure than a strap. No horse will break a sound three-quarter inch rope, though some learn to gnaw it off, and in such cases a light chain is the alternative. For a horse of average size a single stall five to five and a half feet in width is wide enough. It should be sufficient to permit the horse to lie down at ease, but not so wide that it will attempt to turn around in it. Such attempts may lead to serious consequences. Where the stall has a sloping floor, the bedding should be spread so as to equalize the difference and present a level surface. A horse rests much better on a level bed than on one so sloping as to give the constant sensation of slipping into the gutter.

STABLE HABITS AND VICES.

Horses which stand idle in their stalls for any considerable part of the time, are liable to learn unpleasant habits, while other and more serious faults come from innate or acquired viciousness. One

Fig. 46.—INDIA-RUBBER HORSE COVER.

of the worst habits is that of kicking in the stall. This undoubtedly comes at first from nervous restlessness, and finally grows by use to a confirmed habit. Mares are more likely to acquire the habit than geldings. Animals that are perfectly kind and otherwise peaceable will sometimes learn to keep up a steady tattoo at night with their heels against the sides of their stalls. Capped hocks and other injuries are common results, to say nothing of the damage to the stalls. It is useless to punish a horse by whipping for this habit. Indeed, when fully confirmed, it is scarcely ever permanently cured. It may be restrained by suspending a horizontal bar immediately behind the horse, as shown in figure 47. It is hung about a foot above the floor, and when the horse kicks it the bar will fly back, striking its hind legs. The surprised animal will look around to see what struck him, soon becomes tired of the contest, and gives it up as long as the rail hangs there. An empty nail keg may be used instead of the bar. Still it is doubtful if a horse can be permanently broken of the habit.

Pulling at the halter is another bad and even dangerous habit, for if the fastening breaks, the horse is quite likely to get into mischief. Whipping will not cure a horse of this trick, but if the strap or rope, just at the moment when it is drawn taut, is struck a sharp blow with a fork handle or similar stick, midway between the post and the horse, the shock will astonish him. Care must be used not to strike too hard, or it may bring the horse to its knees. A few applications of this will generally prove effective.

Pawing with the fore-feet is a habit induced by the same causes as kicking. It injures the feet, disarranges the bedding, wears out the floor and the shoes. The habit is easily restrained by hobbling the fore-feet together by a strap around the pasterns. But this should be used with caution, as it interferes with the action of the horse in lying down and rising. Another preventive is to nail strips of board an inch thick and two inches wide crosswise of the stall, about a foot apart where the feet strike.

Climbing into the manger with the fore-feet is a trick to which young horses are principally addicted. It is induced by the restlessness which is inevitable from keeping a naturally active, intelligent animal tied down to the dull monotony of a narrow stall. No horse was ever known to do it in a box stall. It is a dangerous habit, for the feet may crash through the bottom of the manger, and broken legs result.

" Weaving," as it is called, consists of a habit of swaying the head rapidly from one side to the other. This, like gnawing and licking the manger, and the other habits named above, comes from a desire to relieve the tedium of confinement and inaction.

The best and in fact the only effective measures, either for prevention or cure of these habits are kindness and a considerate regard for the comfort and well-being of the horse. If there is so little employment for the horse that many hours out of the twenty-four are left between work, feeding, grooming and sleep, it should by all means be given a roomy loose box. No horse with spirit enough to be worth keeping, will stand like an ox, contented and stolid, tied in a narrow stall, hour after hour, with nothing to do. A single horse, kept alone in a stable for family use, is in a worse case than one standing in a large stable with other horses as daily companions. In its yearning for companionship a horse often forms a strong attachment for a dog, or even a cat. Frequent visits to the stable by any members of the household, with caresses, kind words and an occasional lump of sugar or other tidbit, will help to keep

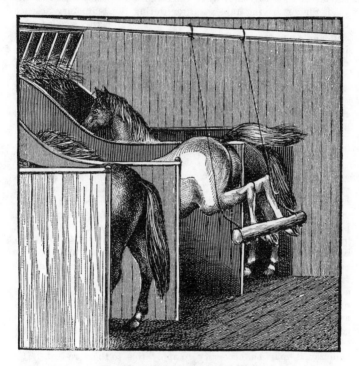

Fig. 47.—BAR FOR KICKING HORSES.

the horse contented, and establish relations which will add greatly to the pleasure of keeping a family horse.

The downright vices of kicking, biting, striking with the fore-feet, like cribbing, are serious disqualifications. A horse which is so vicious as to be dangerous to approach, either in harness or in the stable, is unsafe for general family use, especially where there are children.

DAILY EXERCISE.

One of the indispensable requisites to health and condition of a horse is proper exercise every day. A horse kept for light driving or general family use is too likely to be left standing idle in the stable for days together, when the condition of the weather or the roads render driving unpleasant, or during the temporary absence or illness of the head of the family. Loss of appetite, swelled legs, stiff joints and other evils follow any long continuance of enforced inactivity. As intimated in a previous chapter, the food must be diminished, but that is not enough. Some exercise, if only for half an hour, must be given. If there is an open shed attached to the stable, it affords a place for gentle exercise, but in the absence of such a convenience, it is better for the horse to be led, driven or ridden in any weather, with proper subsequent care, than to stand still all day in its stable.

TURNING TO GRASS AND TAKING UP.

Nothing will freshen a horse more than a run to grass, provided it is done properly. But if one, which has been well fed, blanketed and groomed in a warm stable, is turned out early in spring and made to lie out through the chilly nights, it may end in pneumonia or some other serious if not fatal illness. It is best to give the horse a few hours of daily run to grass at first, with the usual grain ration, and keep it in the stable nights. The time on pasture may be gradually increased, as the horse becomes accustomed to it. Every pasture, whether for horses or other stock, should be provided with shade, under which the animals can find protection from the burning noonday sun of midsummer. If there are no trees, sheds roofed with boards, or even brush, should be constructed. The shoes are to be removed when the horse is first turned out, but if the ground becomes hard and dry during summer, it may be necessary to apply tips to the fore-feet. The pasture should be visited frequently to see that the horse does not become cast or meet with some other casualty. When it is taken up from pasturage the change to stable life and food, with daily work, requires careful and judicious treatment. On this point, Frederick Taylor ("Ballinasloe") says:

"It would be a sure mark of ignorance to take a horse up from grass and feed him with an unlimited quantity of grain and hay at once; these should be given very sparingly at first, particularly the hay; it should for the first week be sprinkled with water to moisten it, and the oats should be mixed with bran, in the proportion of two parts of bran to one of oats, lessening the bran a handful every feed, until it is seen by the consistency of the horse's dunging that he can digest his oats without the inconvenience and dangers of that bane to condition—constipation. This most essential point in the stable management of horses is very much neglected. Grooms seldom take notice of a horse's dung until he is off his feed, and then they either have recourse to some nostrum of their own making up, or wait until inflammation sets in. Some horses are more inclined to constipation than others, hence it is that they all require attention to this point; it is the key to health and condition. The temperature of the stable in which a horse is placed when first taken from the fields should not at first be much increased beyond that of the open air, or the sudden change will probably affect the lungs, and cause inflammation of those organs, or may occasion roaring or broken wind. The horse should for the first few days be placed in a barn, or a roomy loose box, well ventilated, which will allow of his exercising himself, and prevent his legs from swelling, or his feet getting too hot. The temperature should be kept up and increased by degrees, until it is seen to take the requisite effect upon the horse's coat, by causing the long hair to fall off, and a renewal of short hair in its place. This should be encouraged and carefully watched, or, if the temperature gets too high, the hair will fall off in patches, and leave the blue cuticle as bare as the paper I am writing upon—indeed I have, in the course of my experience, seen horses without a particle of hair on their bodies (except the mane and tail), caused by taking them up from grass and placing them at once in a hot stable. I may mention an instance of a clever horse-coper in the midland counties, who prepared a horse by this means, and afterwards sold him at a great price to a showman, who exhibited him as the celebrated ' blue horse ; ' and a queer-looking animal he was too. The clothing should also be very light at first, and the grooming done with a soft brush, or it will cause irritation and itching of the skin. If dieting be carefully attended to, as above recommended, there will be little, if any, necessity for physic. The less physic a horse has the better ; it only weakens his digestive powers, and still further creates a necessity for it, until at last the horse cannot live without it, and will nearly always be amiss. Exercising is the next point to which I shall call attention. At first, a walking pace is quite fast enough, and if the horse is stabled in a loose box, once a day of two hours' duration will be sufficient ; but if in a stall, he ought to be exercised twice a day, morning and evening, and as time progresses—say a week—he may be trotted, and

afterwards galloped, to benefit his wind, and sweat off the superfluous flesh. If the horse has been running at grass with others, it
would be as well to place him in a stable where he will have company, if convenient. Horses are fond of company, and bear separation badly. I have known horses that have been taken up from
others with which they have associated a considerable time, grow
as thin as a rake, and all attempts have failed to get them into condition, until a companion was introduced to keep them company."

DISPOSAL OF MANURE.

The proper management of the solid and liquid manures is a
matter of much importance. With city residents the only question
involved is to keep it cleared away as promptly as possible. Its removal is provided for in most of the large cities by the health authorities. But horse keepers in villages and suburban places usually
have gardens, and the manure, instead of being mere offal to be got
rid of, possesses much practical value. In such situations provision
should be made for storing it where it will be kept from excessive
and destructive fermentation, and so far from the stable that the
offensive odors and gases from the mass will not penetrate it. The
manure should also be kept under cover, or its most valuable elements will leach away. A very good arrangement for disposing of
manure in a manner which will render it wholly inoffensive, while
preserving all its fertilizing properties, is a plank box ten feet long,
six feet wide and two feet deep. This is thoroughly coated with hot
coal-tar inside and out, and sunk two-thirds its depth into the
ground. If in the open air a cover the full size of the top is hinged
to it. For convenience of handling this may be in halves lengthwise and each half hinged to its own side of the box, the ends of
which are a foot the highest in the center, like the gable end of a
building, so that the covers will shed water. If the manure pit is
under a shed no cover will be needed. In such a situation the pit
may be excavated as deeply as desired in the ground, and lined with
cement mortar, instead of wood. The drain from behind the stalls
may be arranged to empty into the manure pit. As the manure is
thrown in, layers of swamp muck or other absorbent, may be alternated every three or four inches. In the absence of any suitable
material, the fresh manure, as it is thrown in, may be freely sprinkled
with land plaster.

The manure from a cow-stable or pig-pen, when there are such
on the premises, may be mixed with the stable manure, with advantage to all. The first named are cold and slow, and tend to check
the excessive heat and fermentation of the horse manure.

CHAPTER V.

CLIPPING, SINGEING AND TRIMMING.

NOTHING connected with horse management has called out more discussion than the practice of clipping and singeing. It is bitterly opposed by many who assert that it is unnatural and cruel to deprive the animal of a portion of its winter covering during the winter. On the other hand, those in its favor claim that so far from rendering the horse more liable to cold, clipping and singeing render him much less so, as any active exercise while wearing a thick coat promotes perspiration, and the moist mat of thick hair becomes cold and clammy as soon as the motion ceases. In fact, the question depends mainly on the time and manner of performing the operation and the subsequent treatment of the horse. There is a right way and a wrong way of doing it, and the differences of opinion have doubtless arisen from the fact that the advocates of the practice have based their opinions upon the proper treatment, and its opponents have seen only its abuses. It cannot be questioned that the thick heavy winter coat is provided by nature to protect the horse from inclemency of the season when it is running at large. But it is wholly unsuited to the stabled and well groomed animal from which rapid work is required. When driven or ridden at a fast pace the horse in its winter coat sweats profusely. When it is pulled up in this state, and made to stand in the open air, or is returned to the stable, with its thick sweaty coat clinging to it, like a wet blanket, the result is not only discomfort, but also liability to colds, coughs and other diseases of the respiratory organs. True, nature provided the heavy winter coat, but a horse which is rapidly driven, and properly stabled, clothed, groomed and cared for, lives under conditions so highly artificial as to materially alter the case. Miss Midy Morgan writes on the subject as follows :

"Why are horses clipped in winter? Why does the shrewd horse owner divest the animal of the covering nature designed for its protection? Horses are clipped for various reasons. In Europe high-bred carriage horses and not infrequently hunters are denuded of a portion of their heavier winter coatings of hair. This change is made to check profuse perspiration and frequently to facilitate the work of the groom. As soon as the chill autumn winds are felt, the best cared for horses show signs of moulting ; their coats become

dull and look wiry ; the summer growth is soon replaced by the
long, thick winter coat. During the season of moulting, fever, more
or less, is present. Horses become languid ; the appetite is morbid ;
and the ability to work is much lessened. These symptoms seldom
continue for more than a few days. Under good care, which com-
prises a change of diet, warm drinks and mashes, with moderate
work, horses come out all right in from fifteen to twenty days. If
a horse on recovering his spirit and showing himself equal to his
usual work grows a heavy coat of hair, the safest way is early in
November to reduce its length one-half ; then in the middle of January again pass the singeing lamp over the horse and reduce the
growth to one-half its natural length. After the first singeing a
stout woolen blanket should be put on the horse ; then if the weather
is severe in January, as it usually is, a light under-blanket should be
added. But how are horses generally clipped? The defenseless
creatures are shorn close to their hides early or late, as their senseless owners take the whim. Then they are either left to shiver and
contract lung or throat diseases, or they are thrust into close hot stables where there is no proper ventilation, and blood poisoning ensues.
Early in the spring the horse-owner finds his horse complaining
with cracked heels, chipped feet, sore eyes or troublesome coughs.
He vows never again to have a horse of his clipped. It was not the
taking off of the animal's winter growth of hair that produced these
woes ; it was the want of proper care afterward that brought about
bad symptoms. When old horses are clipped and a good stable
treatment is not observed, the animal may preserve his appearance of
good health, that is, he may appear cheerful and work well up to his
best form, but his coat will look rusty, feel harsh, and should any
thing go amiss, danger will be close at hand.

  " When farmers decide to clip their horses, let them first provide
due protection ; at least one thin and one heavy blanket for stable
wear, one water-proof quarter blanket, and one water-proof chest
protector. These covers can most profitably be made at home.
Coarse unbleached cotton sheeting, if oiled and allowed to dry, then
oiled again, will be water-proof. These can be readily cut to fit the
individual horses for which they are needed ; then lined with old
blankets or even under the pressure of economy with old pieces of
carpeting ; the sole requisite is that the lining be made of wool. A
quarter-cloth should fit snugly and go over the harness pad with
holes cut in for terrets, and when that obnoxious engine of cruelty,
a check-rein, is used, room must be provided for the hook. When a
quarter-cloth is placed under the back-pad galled backs result, as the
pressure is severe. All outside clothing should be fitted over the

horses, as such protection is needed against rain, snow and sharp winds, so as not to superinduce increased perspiration. There are many of our farm horses whose lives could be made less irksome were they shorn of one-half of their winter's growth of hair, and then judiciously cared for.

" Let no person suppose, however, that should he decide to clip his horses, there will then be no need to dry the weary beasts—thus his care will be less. Better let him bear in mind that a clipped horse stands in absolute need of greater care, and that the benefits to be obtained are an improved condition and better ability to endure fatigue, also a trimness of look pleasing to some. The head and ears of a horse require the most skillful manipulation, as very little hair should be removed ; the legs from the knee down should also be lightly treated. What is necessary is to wash off mud, then rub the legs and especially the heels very dry. A wet or very cold day is precisely the extreme of weather in which no careful groom will clip or singe a horse. A fine bright or (if wet to be waited for) a moderate and a dry day is the weather to select for the operation in which the horse's health and comfort are risked."

Clipping can be properly performed only by an expert, even with the greatly improved implements now used for the purpose. The old-fashioned comb and shears have been superseded by patent horse-clippers, which are made of various patterns adapted to the head, body, and other parts of the horse. A still more advanced invention is the power clipper, of which there are several patterns in the market. These are driven by steam or horse power, or a man at a crank, and the best of them will clip from seven to ten horses in a day. The manner of operation is shown by figure 48, on next page.

No horse should be clipped unless it is in sound health. If it is suffering from any symptoms of a cold or recent indisposition, the clipping must be postponed until health is fully re-established ; nor should any person have a horse clipped until he has provided all the clothing necessary for the clipped animal. Whatever may be said in favor of clipping or singeing under proper circumstances, the practice is utterly indefensible unless the loss of natural protection is made up by subsequent care and artificial protection.

THE TAIL, MANE, ETC.

The tail and mane were given to the horse both for use and beauty. They are means of protection against the attacks of insects upon those parts which the horse cannot reach with its teeth or feet. The tail also seems to act in some way as a sort of rudder when the

horse is in rapid motion. This may readily be seen by observing a
horse when running or trotting. The mane undoubtedly serves to

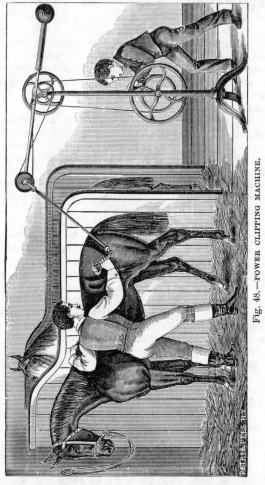

Fig. 48.—POWER CLIPPING MACHINE.

protect the neck and throat from cold and storms. Yet man in his
efforts to "mend nature" deprives the horse of one and sometimes
both of these useful appendages. There is some excuse for shortening

the hair of a saddle horse's tail, for if left at full length it may soil
the legs of the rider.   But there is none for amputating any part of
the sensitive dock.   The old idea that such a practice strengthens
the back-bone has no foundation in fact.   As well might a man
have his ears cropped in the hope that it would increase his brain-
power.   Nicking or pricking is a painful operation, performed for
the purpose of making the horse carry his tail more elevated.   It consists of cutting deeply into the under side of the tail, and then keeping the wounds open and inflamed by fastening the tail in an elevated position.   The operation is so severe that lockjaw sometimes ensues.   The desired object can be attained in a much more humane
way by fastening the tail to a cord running through pulleys and
having a weight at the other end.   The pulleys are hung from the

Fig. 49.—MANE DRAG.

ceiling in the rear of the stall, one directly over the croup of the horse
and the other at a sufficient distance to keep the weight away from
the horse.   One pound is heavy enough for the weight the first
week, but it is increased from week to week.   The tail is kept elevated by this means for one hour each day, increasing the time gradually to three hours, until it remains permanently set up.

No good excuse has ever been offered for roaching the mane.   So
far from improving the horse's appearance it gives the neck an ugly,
rough aspect, and serves no possible good purpose.   If it is thicker
than is desirable, the mane may be thinned by the use of the drag,
shown at figure 49.   This will remove a portion of the hair at each
dressing without disfigurement.   It is also used for thinning the
hair of the tail.

It is a very common practice to clip away the long hair around
and above the pasterns.   The custom is a pernicious one, and a prolific source of mud fever, scratches, and grease.   This hair is nature's
own provision against the irritating effects of mud.   Clipping it is
an evil, because the thick hair, to a great extent, would prevent actual contact of particles of mud, sand, and manure with the skin.   It
naturally acts as a kind of percolator, or filter, passing the liquid,
but rejecting the solid particles.   It also acts as a sort of blanket to
retain the animal heat in the extremities.   Thoroughbred horses

have very little of this hair, while with English and Scotch draft horses a thick growth is a conspicuous characteristic of the breed.

The long hair around the muzzle and nostrils doubtless act in some degree similar to the whiskers of a cat, as organs of perception, and their removal is injurious. An excess of coarse hairs in those parts indicates low breeding, and is never seen in a thoroughbred. But if shorn off, they will soon grow out again harsher than at first. The long hairs above and below the eyes serve a very important purpose in protecting those delicate organs, and should never be interfered with. The growth of fine hair inside the ears is there for their protection. If it becomes so long as to protrude beyond the outer edges of the ear, the ends may be shortened, but it should never be cut out from the inside of the ears.

CHAPTER VI.

ON THE ROAD.

WE make no suggestions here in regard to training an unbroken colt to harness or saddle, further than to remark that the work of education should begin with the foal before it is a month old. To let a youngster run wild at its own sweet will until it has attained nearly full growth and strength, and then attempt to "break" it by sheer brute force, is not the best way to obtain a kindly, well-trained horse. But the details of training up a foal in the way it should go are outside the scope of this work. The family horse is presumed to have been sufficiently well advanced to go quietly in harness or under saddle. True, the standard of equine education is not very high in this country, and as Herbert remarks, "if a horse will carry its rider without throwing him over its head, or draw him in his wagon or buggy without kicking it to shivers; if it will go off at a walk, increase its speed to the top of his gait, and stop again when pulled upon, without running away; if it will hold back going down hill, and will not balk going up hill; and more particularly, if it will stand at a door without tying, it is held to be fully broken." A horse which comes up even to that standard, though it is far from being "nothing more than a living and spirited automaton in the hands of its rider or driver," does very well for the practical purposes of a family horse. If treated, as every horse should be, with perfect kindness and patience, yet with inflexible firmness to insure obedience, such a horse will soon learn to understand the wishes of its driver by the very tones of his voice, or the touch of his hand upon the reins.

It is essential that every part of the harness shall fit the horse so that there shall be no chafing or undue pressure in any part. For a horse to go with a collar so loose as to chafe or so tight as to pinch, the girths compressing its chest too closely, the breeching interfering with free action of its hind legs, or the crupper galling it under the tail, is like a man's trying to run a foot-race with gravel in his shoes. In harnessing the horse, it should first be led out of its stall, the collar—if one is worn—turned upside down and slipped over the horse's head. Then the harness is laid quietly on him, not thrown forcibly. The hames are adjusted to their place on the collar, the crupper put in place and buckled to the back-strap, and the inner girth drawn not too snugly, and also buckled. If a breast-collar is used, the operations around the neck are much simplified.

The horse should never be started on a full stomach for a long or hard drive. A portion of the ordinary hay ration may be with-held and the grain slightly increased. To drive well is an accom-plishment which requires observation, steady nerves and practice. A good driver will never start the horse with a shout and a blow, or even a crack of the whip. But gathering the reins firmly in hand, he will start off quietly with a word or a chirrup. He will allow the horse to go very moderately at first, gradually increasing the pace, as the animal becomes warmed to the work. He will hold the reins just tight enough to feel the horse's mouth, but not to bruise and saw it with the bits. He will sit straight, keeping a constant alert lookout on the horse, at the same time observing the road ahead so as to avoid every serious obstacle, and turn out at the proper time for those he meets. It is essential that the horse shall have what is called a good mouth, sensitive to the slightest pressure of the bit. The driver needs to maintain a steady, even tension of the reins. Jerking one rein and then the other, slapping the horse's back with them, and keeping up a constant volley of words, are all bad prac-tices which worry and irritate the horse.

On a drive of any considerable length, it is far better to maintain a good steady pace after the horse is fairly warmed to the work, than to go by fits and starts, spurting for a time at the utmost speed which can be got out of the horse, and then jogging along at a walk. When driving for pleasure or business with a light wagon, and a fairly good horse, an average gait of eight miles an hour may be kept up for a long time, with less wear to the horse than a jerky and fitful pace. But to quote again from Herbert: "In speaking of driving at an equal pace, we would not, of course, be understood to mean that horses should be driven at the same gait and speed over all roads, and over ground of all natures. Far from it. A good driver will never, perhaps, have his horse going at exactly the same rate for any two consecutive twenty minutes. Over a dead level, the hardest of all things except a long continuous ascent of miles, he will spare his horses. Over a rolling road he will hold them hard in hand as he crosses the top and descends the first steep pitch of a down-grade, will swing them down the remainder at a pace which will carry them across the intervening flat and half way up the suc-

(81–82)

THE BLACK GELDING GUY, SIRED BY KENTUCKY PRINCE, DAM BY SEELY'S AMERICAN STAR.

ceeding hill, and will catch them in hand again, and hold them hard over the top, as before."

When being driven either for business or pleasure, horses should be watered at intervals of an hour or so, but not more than half a bucketful at once. When going all day, they should be watered and fed at least once during the day, and light feeds at frequent intervals are better. A feed eaten from a nose-bag, while standing in the harness, is sometimes the best that can be given, under the circumstances. But when it is possible to relieve the horse of its harness, put it in a stall and make it comfortable while taking its mid-day rations, it will be far better prepared to go during the remainder of the day.

A horse that has spirit enough to go with any satisfaction to its driver rarely needs the whip. The writer once had a young horse which he drove for months at a time without taking the whip from the socket. With keen intelligence and a high spirit, the horse was quick to comprehend what was expected of him, and eager to perform it. Upon such a horse a blow, save in some extreme emergency, is a barbarous outrage. There are sluggish or refractory horses which sometimes require the lash, but it should never be applied to urge forward a jaded or exhausted animal. The word "whoa" should never be used except when the horse is desired to come to a full stop. He should be taught the meaning of that word as well as "back" and "steady," and made to obey them.

Driving a spirited horse, with good trotting action, is one of the keenest and most exhilarating pleasures in the world. Such a horse requires the best of care in the stable, especially its feet. In a well-fitting harness, to a strong, light road-wagon, with a smooth road and a skillful driver, it will show the very "poetry of motion." "The driver takes a line in each hand," says Mr. H. W. Rugg, "and the circuit is complete. He signals with so light a touch that his partner for the ride cannot detect them, yet the response is prompt and certain. As he flies along the smooth roadway so evenly he feels the thrill in every nerve. A horse like that would go at a rattling pace until it dropped down a wreck. The good driver will always keep something back for an emergency. He will know when to let up, then watch for the first signal of distress, the swinging head, the changing gait, the labored breath. A great many overdrive the first half of their ride, and spend the time of the latter half in regret-ting it. Before starting out try and determine not only the route, but the time it is proposed to be on the road. At the start let the horse take an easy gait, and keep him cool as possible. If inclined to fret, talk to him in an easy tone, using few words, but use the word 'whoa' only for a full stop. Keep it in mind that the strong pull at the bit frets and tires the horse as well as the driver. Another objection urged is that spirited horses pull so hard on the bit that it is more work than pleasure to drive them. This is largely the fault of early training to trot their best for a single mile. To change the gait or style of going is no easy task, but with patience and perseverance it can be done. For this purpose take some quiet road and with a good, smooth mile ahead, let the horse come up to his average gait as easily as possible; then, in going that mile, gradually reduce the pull ten per cent. It will be better for ultimate success if it is only reduced the merest trifle than have the horse feel the slack and start off for a spurt. Should the horse from any cause become excited when doing this work, let him walk it off first. Having once established an easy road-gait for the horse, do not let others fool with it, as one master is enough for any fine horse. Many boys think there is some great secret in driving, by which horses can be made to trot fast almost at will. To obtain this, they haunt the trotting courses, catch at every word of the trainers and stablemen, and thus lose much time. Such persons may be met driving on the road with bent bodies and outstretched arms, shouting in jockey style, in a hopeless struggle to make a hundred-dollar horse show a five-hundred-dollar gait. With as much reason they might stand by and watch a smoking dunghill, expecting to see the eruption of an Ætna or a Vesuvius."

Driving a pair is well described by Stonehenge as follows : " In driving a pair, the great art consists in putting them together so as to draw equally, and to step together. To do this well, the horses must match in action and temper, two slugs being much better than a free-tempered horse with a slug; because, in this case, the whip applied to the one only makes the other more free, and as a consequence it is impossible to make them draw equally. In some cases where two horses are exactly equally matched, the coupling-reins must both be of equal length ; but this is seldom the case; and when they do not do an equal amount of work, the coupling-rein of the free one must be taken up, and that of the idle horse let out. In watching the working of the two horses the pole-pieces should always be the guide ; and if both are slack, with the end of the pole steady, and neither horse shouldering it, the driver may rest contented that his horses are each doing their share ; if, however, the pole is shouldered by either, that horse is a rogue, and is making the other do more than his share, keeping the pole straight by the pressure of his shoulder, instead of pulling at the traces. On the other hand, if either horse is pulling away from the pole, and straining at the pole-piece, he is doing more than his share, and his coupling-rein must be taken in accordingly. Sometimes both shoulder the pole, or spread from it, which are equally unsightly habits, and may generally be cured by an alteration of the coupling-reins of both horses, letting them out for shouldering, and taking them in for its opposite bad habit. The reins are held in the same way for double-harness as for single. In driving a pair, it should always be remembered that there are two methods of driving round a curve, one by pulling the inside rein, and the other by hitting the outside horse, and these two should generally be combined, graduating the use of the whip by the thinness of the skin of the horse. In all cases the whip is required in double-harness, if not to drive horses when thoroughly put together, yet to make them pull equally ; and there are very few pairs which do not occasionally want a little reminding of their duties. A constant change from one side to the other is a prevention of those tricks and bad habits which horses get into if they are kept to one side only. The coachman should, therefore, change them every now and then, and back again, so as to make what was a puller from the pole, rather bear towards it than otherwise when put on the other side."

It is better to drive the last mile slowly, to let the horse cool off. On returning to the stable the mouth should be sponged out, the feet carefully examined to see that no large or small stones have lodged between the shoe and the sole, and the horse dressed, as indicated at page 62. If the harness is left on until the horse becomes partially cooled, there will be less liability of galls under the collar and back-pad.

BAD HABITS AND TRICKS.

Most if not all the evil ways which horses show in harness and under saddle are the result of bad management. If the horses of the future are to be saved from vices and ailments, the work will have to begin with the men who are to have them in charge. But at present we can only guard against the bad habits which horses now in hand have acquired or inherited.

Balking is one of the most annoying tricks of a horse, and which is almost invariably the result of over-loading or harshness. Spirited, well-bred horses are more liable to balk than sluggish ones. If asked to draw a load beyond its strength, or started suddenly with a flourish and perhaps a blow of the whip, an intelligent, nervous horse becomes discouraged, and a spirit of opposition is aroused within it at once. After the habit has become confirmed the animal will, at a

harsh, angry word, or other provocation, refuse to draw anything,
balking even when going down hill with an empty buggy. Beating
or harsh measures of any kind only aggravate the matter. The
horse seems to think he has a grievance, and will not start while
he broods over it. Any mild measure which will divert his attention will break the spell. One ingenious driver pulled down the left
ear of his balky horse, and tied it there. It was a new experience to
the animal, and he forgot his grievance, and started along without
further trouble. But the satisfaction of the driver was somewhat
modified when he found that the horse thereafter refused to start until
his left ear was duly tied down to the headstall. A method which

Fig. 51.—WIRE REIN-HOLDER.

is used with some success is to unhitch the balking horse at once
from the vehicle and lead him round several times in a narrow circle.
He is then replaced in the shafts, and goes on without further
trouble. Another method is to go to the horse's head, speak kindly
to him, then lift one of his feet and tap it lightly a few times with a
stone. There are many other devices with the same object which
will suggest themselves to any one driving balky horses. But if a
spirited and intelligent horse is over-loaded and knows it, all these
little artifices are in vain. Balking is not the result of "equine
epilepsy," as one eminent writer would have it, nor of "cussedness,"
as many people suppose. It is a dumb protest against over-loading
and abuse. If there were no unskillful, thoughtless or unkind drivers, there would be no balky horses.

Catching the lines under the tail is an unpleasant trick, and
often the first move toward a runaway. If the seat is high enough,

and the lines are held properly, it cannot occur. But in phaetons and other low-seated vehicles, it is not easy to hold the lines out of reach of a practiced tail-swinger. When it does occur, the best way is to reach forward, seize the tail and liberate the lines at once. Figure 51 shows a serviceable device for prevention. It consists of a double loop A of copper wire, fastened to the brace-strap at its junction with the back-strap. The reins are passed each through one of the loops in the wire.

Hanging out the tongue is a ridiculous habit, which comes from various causes. A very effective preventive is the use of the bit shown in figure 52. It is made of leather and in the back part of it are fastened two small screw-eyes a little more than two inches apart. A piece of stiff No. 10 wire, seven inches long, is bent to two right angles, and an eye turned in each end and inserted in the

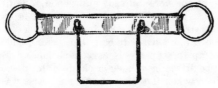

Fig. 52.—HOME-MADE LEATHER TONGUE-BIT.

screw-eyes as shown. This lies lightly on the tongue, yet prevents it from being thrust over the bit and hanging out of the mouth. Various patterns of tongue-bits are in the market, each having a plate or loop attached to the bit and resting on the tongue. But the home-made leather bit is as serviceable as any.

Shying is in most cases caused by imperfect vision. Some horses are naturally "buck-eyed," as it is called, the lens of the eye being too convex, as in short-sighted persons. An English gentleman who owned a horse of this kind had a pair of spectacles fitted to its eyes, which were worn with much satisfaction to both driver and horse, the latter never showing any further disposition to shy. Other horses have their vision impaired by standing in dark or foul stables, wearing badly-fitting blinders, or by getting hay-seed and dirt in their eyes when feeding from high racks. A horse is more easily frightened by an object which it cannot make out than one which it can see plainly. It will stand quietly near a railroad station, and regard the hissing, screeching engines with perfect indifference, but will spring aside in an agony of terror if a white calf or a man in his shirt sleeves appears suddenly in a wayside field which it is being driven past. Besides this involuntary shying from nervousness and fright, some horses learn to shy from pure mischief. In any case the driver should keep the horses teady, and get it past the object of its fright. An encouraging word, all the while holding the horse firmly in hand will generally restore its confidence. Forcing the horse up to the object only increases its panic, and in no case should the lash or any severity be used after it has got past the object.

Running away, when it becomes a confirmed habit, is one of the worst a family horse can have. It is shying carried to the bitter end. The sudden opening of an umbrella, the discharge of fire-arms, some other alarming sight or sound, or the vehicle running upon its hind legs, frightens the horse, which bolts and runs. The driver, as much panic-stricken as the horse, jerks nervously on the reins, saws on the bit, and rapidly yells " whoa! " communicating his own terror to that of the horse, already quite enough, until the animal is worked into frenzy. If the run does not end in some frightful catastrophe, it is through sheer good fortune. After one such experience the horse is more liable to bolt than before, and a few repetitions of it completely upsets his nervous balance. Such a horse should never be driven by women or children, for no one knows the day or the hour when it will start on a mad race. A strong, self-possessed man often drives such a horse for years without trouble, for a horse never runs away while it has confidence in its driver. A few words, in a reassuring tone, when the horse first bolts, will often bring him to reason and avert a catastrophe.

CHAPTER VII.

RIDING ON HORSEBACK.

In the colonial days the family horse rendered more service under the saddle and the pillion than in harness. When the mill was to be visited, the good man started on horseback, having behind him a bag with the grist in one end and a stone in the other, to preserve the balance. On Sunday he went to meeting in the same style, save that it was the good wife mounted behind him on a pillion. Perchance it was one of the younger men with his Priscilla on the pillion ; and it is highly probable that neither would have exchanged their double mount for the best pair of park hacks that ever looked through bridles. But as railroads and passable wagon-roads came in, saddles went out, until they could scarcely be found on the farm, unless it was among the forgotten rubbish of some dusty corner. Riding continued longer in the South than in the North, but even there it became more and more neglected.

But during the life of the present generation there has been a great revival of interest in equestri-anism. Much of this was doubtless caused by the war, in which over 500,000 horses were employed in the cavalry on both sides, in addition to those ridden by mounted officers. Thousands of men learned to ride, who would have never sat in a sad-dle but for the war, and at its close these men carried home with them a taste for riding, which diffused itself, and has continued ever since. There is no more healthful, ani-mating or invigorating exercise for men or women, than riding.

Fig. 53 —PLAIN SNAFFLE BIT.

THE EQUIPMENTS.

The first consideration in preparing for equestrian exercise is the outfit. The bridle should be of plain russet leather, free from all frippery in the way of useless ornaments. The bit is a matter of great importance. There is an infinite variety of bits, and whole volumes have been written on the subject. The simplest form is the common snaffle, shown in figure 53. It is provided with guards to keep it from being pulled into the horse's mouth. The double-jointed snaffle bit has a short link in place of a single joint in the middle. Snaffle bits are sometimes made of twisted wire, but they are severe and cut the mouth. The curb bit, shown in figure 54, has a bend in the middle, called the port, which, by the action of the reins, is pressed upward against the sensitive bars in the roof of the mouth. These bits have, attached to the upper part of the side-bars, a curb-chain, which presses against the lower jaw. The Pelham bit, illustrated in figure 55, is a combination of the snaffle and curb. In the middle is a hinge-joint, instead of the link-joint of the snaffle. The bridoon, figure 56, is a plain jointed bit, like a snaffle, without the side-

Fig. 54.—BAUCHER CURB BIT.

bars. For riding it is used in connection with a curb bit, and the arrangement is very effective. Each of them has separate side-straps to the head-stall and separate reins. The bridoon is worn inside of the curb bit, or it will press the latter and cause chafing.

Fig. 55.—PELHAM BIT.

The reins of the bridoon and curb bits are never to be held tight at the same time. The bridoon reins are generally sufficient for straightway riding, and when the curb is needed, the bridoon reins are relaxed.

Equal in importance to the choice of a proper bit is that of the saddle. The English park saddle, illustrated in figure 57, is the one almost universally employed in England and in all but the more primitive portions of the United States. The best are made of pigskin. They are padded inside, except a space directly over the horse's spine and withers, which is left chambered, to prevent direct pressure upon the spine. A ring is fastened to either side, near the top, in front, to which the breast-plate straps may, if desired, be attached. The girths are of webbing, or better, of hair. The stirrup-leathers run through bars which, in all well-made saddles, are now made to close with a spring clasp, which opens and liberates the stirrup in case the rider is thrown and his foot becomes entangled in the stirrup. The stirrups are of iron or steel, large enough to allow the foot to enter. The bottom, upon which the foot rests, should be an inch and a half broad. It is either roughed up or fitted with an India-rubber pad.

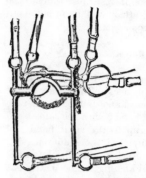

Fig. 56.—BIT AND BRIDOON.

The breast-plate is used only in hunting across hilly country, and even then is rarely needed.

The standing martingale is buckled to the bridle, and is a nuisance. The running or ring martingales terminate in rings, which are slipped over the reins, upon which they slide freely.

For those who have learned how to use them, spurs are of great asssitance to urge the horse forward, and also in training and controling him. But they must never be used harshly, and horses are often excited and maddened by untaught, indiscriminate spurring. Inexperienced riders had better not wear spurs. A good riding-whip is quite sufficient for ordinary purposes. It should be carried in the right hand, butt uppermost.

In bridling and saddling the horse, all parts of the equipments should fit properly. The side-straps of the bridle should be long enough to hold the bits in place without drawing the lips out of shape. The saddle-girths should not be drawn so tight as to suffocate and distress the horse. The stirrup

Fig. 57.—PARK SADDLE.

leathers should be of such length that the steps of the stirrup will just touch the heel of the rider above the sole. This may be approximately measured by the rider before mounting. Standing beside the horse, he takes the stirrup in his left hand and places it in his right arm-pit, with the arm and palm of the right hand lying lengthwise of the leather. If the bar in which it rests just touches the first joints of the middle finger, the leathers will be found about the right length for a man of average proportions.

MOUNTING AND RIDING.

Approach the horse on the near side quietly, but without showing trepidation, speak to him and pat his neck. Then draw on the reins until you feel the horse's mouth, but do not pull on them, take them in the last three fingers of the left hand ; with the same hand seize a lock of the mane, take the stirrup by the right hand and insert the left foot ; then seize the pommel of the saddle, passing the fingers under it with the thumb outside ; press the left knee slightly against the horse's side, to avoid kicking him with the left foot ; then spring lightly upward, until the left leg is nearly straight ; then throw the right foot over the pommel without bending the knee, and settle into your seat. Some riding-masters prefer to place the right hand upon the cantle, rather than the pommel of the saddle. This makes it easier to spring from the ground, but the hand must be changed to the pommel before the right leg can swing into place. In dismounting the same movements are reversed. If a spur is worn, care must be used not to touch the horse with it when swinging the right foot across the horse's back.

The rider must sit erect, well down in the saddle, square to the front, with the chest well thrown out and the shoulders back. The thighs and knees grip the saddle, and the legs below the knees hang free. The toes must be turned neither out nor in, but straight forward, leaving the feet parallel with the horse's side. It is the grip of the knees that enables a good rider to maintain his seat under all conditions. The reins are to guide the horse, and not in any degree to assist the rider in holding on. The arms rest with the elbows just touching the sides, without stiffness. From the elbows outward the arms are horizontal. For ordinary riding the reins are held in the left hand, being brought through between the fingers, the ends folded back over the top of the first finger, and kept there by the thumb, which points towards the horse's ears. The right hand rests by the right hip, with the whip hanging down. In riding across country, or where it is difficult, both hands are employed to hold the reins. " The legs," says Herbert, " are no less important in guiding and assisting the horse in his movements, than are the hands. A uniform pressure of both legs tends to bring the horse's hind feet forward, or to give a forward motion to his body. The pressure of one leg, placed behind the girths, tends to turn the croup around the fore legs from that side. An equal pressure of both legs differently placed, and delicately aided by the hand, tends to turn the horse around his center of gravity, and by a combination of these aids, which require as much management of the legs, as in that of the hands, the horse in his movements may be entirely submissive to the will of the rider."

The so-called "natural gaits" are the walk, the trot, the gallop and the canter. No saddle horse is worth having unless he be a good fast walker. A slow walking horse is a vexation to the spirit, and a horse whose walk is so slow that in order to keep up with his fellows he must resort to the jog trot, is a quadruped whose proper vocation is with the plow. Three miles and a half an hour is as slow as the saddle horse ought to be allowed to walk. Four miles is a good honest swinging gait, and every roadster ought to be able to take it. The trot is the most natural and usual gait of English hackneys and cabs, and has become the fashionable thing in this country among those who ride mainly for exercise. Military riders have to maintain a "close seat," that is, sit square down in the saddle. With such a seat trotting causes great weariness, not to speak of stiff joints and abraded cuticles. The English method, which is also practiced in this country, is to spring from the saddle at every alternate step of the horse. This makes it much easier for both rider and horse. The knees are used as a pivot, aided by a slight pressure upon the stirrups. The tendency which should be avoided, is to lean forward at each spring, as if about to dive over the horse's head. Another ludicrous practice is to swing the elbows, like flapping wings. The gallop and canter are easy and graceful gaits. The rider sits down in the saddle, grasping the horse with the thighs and knees, but not so closely as to distress it. He leans a little forward and conforms to the motions of the horse. The gallop and the run are the horse's extreme gaits, and those in which, when in health and spirits, he most rejoices. In the gallop the legs on the right side move in advance of those on the left or those on the left side in advance of those on the right. When turning, the fore-leg on the side toward which the turn is made should strike the ground in advance of the other. The canter or lope is, especially for ladies' horses, a delightful gait to ride, and one easily taught. When a horse "lopes" springingly and gracefully it is the pleasantest gait to ride, and the one in which, for park and city purposes, a woman appears to the very best advantage. It is simply the gallop slowed down or modified.

The fox-trot is an artificial gait, much cultivated in the West and South. It is not encouraged by the riding-masters, but is a very easy, comfortable gait, which can be kept up all day with little fatigue to the rider.

Jumping must be learned by degrees. The English method is to begin while the horse is young, and coax it to leap, by holding

out its grain in plain view on the opposite side of the hurdle. This practise is followed six months, gradually increasing the height of the bar, before a rider is placed on the back. An older horse may be taught by first leading it over a low bar on a walk. The bar is raised from time to time, the horse still being led slowly over it. Then it is led to it at a run, man and horse both jumping over it. When the horse is accustomed to jump with no one on his back he may be mounted, and sent over a low bar at first, gradually increasing the height. By no means ride him up to a jump which is higher than he is willing to take, as it will discourage him. The standing leap should first be practiced. Then trot or canter to the jump, take the reins

Fig. 58.—AMERICAN SADDLE.

in both hands, sit down firmly in the saddle, and from the moment the horse rises for the jump do nothing with knees, hands or voice which can confuse him. Hold firmly with the knees, lean backward, give the horse the reins as he rises, and be ready to hold them firmly and help him recover as soon as he lands.

COW-BOY RIDING.

Throughout the remote West and Southwest, wherever cattle range in great herds, there is a class of riders whose style may be regarded as peculiarly American. Instead of the English saddle, they use one more like that illustrated in figure 58. The tree is covered with heavy oil-dressed leather, the stirrups are of bent hickory, set so far back that the rider is nearly as erect as if standing on the ground. A broncho with one of these ponderous saddles fastened on his back by a hair "cincha," and the remainder of the outfit equally unique, presents a striking contrast with a natty, bang-tailed hackney, equipped in Eastern style. But uncouth as the pony and rider may look to Eastern eyes, there are no finer riders in the world than cow-boys. They sit their vicious, half-tamed ponies with easy grace and confidence. There is small need of knee-grip, for they maintain their balance while loping over ground hollow with prairie-dog holes, and can swing over to one side so low as to pick a hat from the ground while going at a gallop.

LADY EQUESTRIANISM.

There is no exercise more healthful, delightful or lady-like than horseback riding. Saddles for ladies' use are now mostly made without the old-fashioned right hand horn, but with a second horn on the left side, called the leaping horn or crutch, as shown in figure 59. The right leg rests on the upper horn, and the left knee is held firmly against the lower one, the left foot being in the stirrup. This enables the fair rider to hold on with a firmer grip than a man can secure with his knees. The stirrup leather must be hung from a safety-bar as in men's saddles. The stirrup has an iron sole, and in most cases a leather slipper covering the toes. For ladies' riding, some more powerful bit is required than a plain snaffle. The best is either a Pelham (figure 55) or the bit and bridoon (figure 56). The latter is preferable in riding a spirited horse, for they are not only more complete, but in case one bit breaks, another remains. The whip should be rather long and heavy, for it must be used in place of a spur.

Fig. 59.—LADIES' SADDLE.

Riding costumes for ladies have been greatly improved within a few years. The habit comes but little below the feet, the waist fitting the figure neatly, and the plain sleeves large enough for ease and freedom. Turkish trousers, of the same material as the habit, come down to the tops of the high boots. If the weather is such as to demand more protection, a divided skirt of quilted silk is worn. Close fitting sacks of sealskin or similar fur are allowable. Gauntlets are worn of fine buckskin or dogskin. The hat is a matter of taste and choice. The hair should be dressed in a firm, plain style. Chains, bracelets and any conspicuous display of jewelry are vulgar and out of place on horseback.

Some one must hold the horse by the head, while another assists the lady to mount. With her right hand holding the whip and reins on the pommel, she lifts her skirt from the ground with her left. The gentleman stoops and takes the lady's left foot in his right hand, while he holds the horse's mane with his left. The lady, releasing the skirt, places her left hand on the gentleman's shoulder, springs upward to straighten the left knee, and the gentleman lifts her high enough to enable her to settle easily into the saddle. She then adjusts her skirt, places her right knee over the pommel, and the gentleman places her left foot in the stirrup. "The lady," says Anderson, "should sit upon the horse so that her weight will fall perpendicularly to the back of the horse ; her face directly to the front, her shoulders drawn back, and her elbows held to her sides. She will permit her body, from the hips upward, to bend with the motions of the horse, in order that she may preserve her balance. The reins are to be held in the manner prescribed for men, the hand in front of the body, and in a line with the elbow. The whip is to be carried in the right hand, with the point toward the ground. The horse should never be struck with the whip upon the head, neck, or shoulder. To apply it upon those parts will teach him to swerve, and render him nervous at the motions of the rider. In a lady's hand the whip simply takes the place of a spur for the right side. The horns of the saddle, the superfluous one at the right being dispensed with, should be of such lengths and curvatures as will suit the rider. The right leg will hold the upright horn close in the bend in the knee, by such a pressure as the action of the horse or other circumstances will dictate. The left foot will be thrust into the stirrup to the ball of the foot, and the heel will, as a rule, be carried down ; but when the heel is elevated the upper part of the left knee should find support in the side-horn, and for that end the stirrup-leather will be given such a length as will permit this. By the grasp given by the elevation of the left knee from the stirrup and the embrace upon the upright horn by the right leg, the rider will have as strong a seat as her strength can afford ; and with a proper balance she will not be likely to find a horse that will unseat her."

CHAPTER VIII.

HARNESS AND VEHICLES.

A MATTER of the first importance is to have well-made and well-fitting harness, and every part of the wagon and outfit in good order. The head-stall should be adjusted to bring the bit down to the angle of the mouth, so as to rest easily there, instead of drawing it into a sardonic grin, as it will if too short. Blinders are an abomination on a single horse. Every argument in favor of using them with a pair of horses falls to the ground if applied to a single one. There is absolutely no more reason for using blinders on a horse in harness, than on one under saddle. Fancy a party of red-coated gentlemen galloping across the country with blinders on their horses! Yet habit alone has taught us to tolerate them in one case more than in the other. If a horse is driven without blinders from the first, he will go better single without them. They afford no protection against shying, for the horse never shies at an object which he fully recognizes. They often cause blindness by pressure against the eyes, and by retaining dust and heat. If a horse has long been accustomed to blinders, it is not advisable to leave them off all at once. The flaring half-blinders may be substituted, until the animal regains the natural use of its eyes.

The check-rein is a source of great abuse and suffering. For a short overdraw check, which holds the horse's head in a star-gazing position, with the nose pointed forward, there is no excuse whatever. A check of any kind should never be reined uncomfortably high. It tires and stiffens the neck and destroys all elasticity and freedom. The horse is surer footed when its head is free, and if it should stumble, throwing its head down greatly assists in recovering. It is absurd to suppose that a tight check-rein helps to hold up a horse. It is like a man's trying to lift himself off the ground by tightening his suspenders. A writer of acknowledged authority says: " One of the most prevalent abuses ; one that causes the greatest torture ; one that diminishes the value and shortens the lives of more horses than any other, is perhaps the use of over-checks tightly drawn during long intervals, and at times when the horse most needs freedom for the full exercise of his lungs, nerves and muscles of the neck and head. Any thoughtful person who examines the anatomical structure of the head and neck of the horse, must be impressed with the great strain upon these nerves and muscles required by nature, even when their normal liberty or freedom are undisturbed or perturbed by artificial devices. That over-checking is often the initial cause of inflammation of the muscles and even the brain there is little doubt. If this be true, can it be doubted that this habit of tight over-checking (or tight reining) as practiced by many persons, often contributes to the virulence of spinal meningitis, neuralgia, rheumatism, thumps, apoplexy and paralysis. etc."

Harsh bits are not only cruel, but unwise; though they may be very effective at first, they ultimately make the mouth hard and callous. Frosty iron bits inflict torture and permanent injury, and no one but a brutally careless person would ever thrust them into a

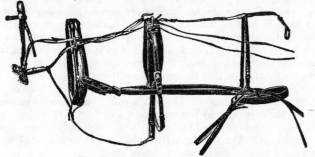

Fig. 60.—ENGLISH COLLAR HARNESS.

horse's mouth. There are now in market several patterns of bits covered with leather or India-rubber, which are better, at least in cold weather, than metallic bits of any kind.

Every part of the harness must fit snugly, but with ease and comfort. This point is often overlooked in changing a harness from one horse to another. For general family purposes and heavy work of all kinds, the English collar and hames, illustrated in figure 60, are the best. This distributes the draught equally over the shoulders and breast. The collar should conform to the horse not only in size, but in shape. A collar which is too loose chafes, and undue pressure at any point galls the shoulders. There should be space inside the lower end of the collar to admit the fingers between it and the windpipe. All parts of the collar that press upon the shoulders must be kept clean and flexible, and not allowed to become encrusted with perspiration and dirt. Galled shoulders are very prevalent with horses performing heavy work. The liability is greatest with horses working on level ground. The long-continued, unchanging pressure on the same spot, is much more severe than the shifting which occurs in going up-hill and down. For horses employed at heavy work in warm weather, the device shown in figure 61 affords a very effective protection. It consists of a clean cotton cloth, well smeared with pure tallow, wrapped around the collar, and the ends lightly stitched together. It is to fit so lightly as to go under the harness, which aids to hold it in place. A small proportion of beeswax first melted with the tallow will render the application more lasting. Collar-pads are also useful for the same purpose. They consist of thin quilted pads, worn under the collar. The martingale holds the collar from pressing upward and choking the horse, as it is liable to do in going up-hill, or drawing a load, especially if the shoulders are very sloping. The belly-bands should be buckled just tightly enough for a snug fit, but not to constrict the chest and prevent its proper expansion as the horse inflates his lungs.

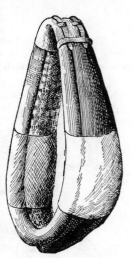

Fig. 61.—SHOULDER PROTECTOR.

For light driving the breast collar, shown at figure 62, may be used. This should be fitted well up from the point of the shoulder, as high as possible, without choking. An inch at least should be allowed on each side to accommodate the natural rise of the neck when moving. The pad is to be broad and soft, with the under-girth drawn snug, not tight, the outer girth loose enough to allow for the movement of thills. If a cart is used, there must be a safety-strap, as the outer girth must be drawn tight. The breeching should fit well up on the quarters, as high as possible and not work up over them. The breast collar has a very neat appearance, but is suitable only for light work. It rests directly upon the point of motion, where any heavy pressure must interfere with freedom of action. Moreover, it lies directly across the windpipe, and horses are sometimes choked down when drawing a heavy load up a hill in a breast collar. Yet, for the trotting ring or any light work in single harness, it is preferable to the English collar. It shows off a good horse to the best advantage, and is also useful as a change when the shoulders have become galled from working in a collar.

All expensive ornamentation is in bad taste. Nothing shows a good horse to greater advantage than a neat, well-fitting harness in perfect order, and free from excessive display of burnished metal or other useless decorations.

CARE OF HARNESS.

The harness should be kept in a closet or other place protected from dust, and wholly apart from the odors of the stable. The ammoniacal gases which cause the smell of stables are extremely

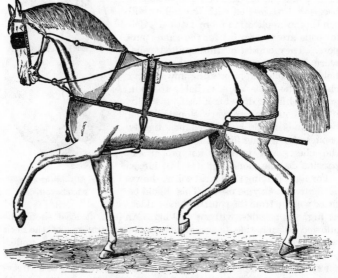

Fig. 62.—BREAST-COLLAR HARNESS.

caustic and destructive to leather. Every time it is used, the harness should be wiped when taken off the horse, all sweaty straps being rubbed with a damp sponge, and then the whole rubbed dry with chamois skin or a dry cloth. If this is neglected, it soon becomes gummed up and requires a thorough cleaning. The straps should not be soaked in water, as it hardens the leather, but rubbed with a sponge dampened in warm soap-suds, then wiped dry and oiled. If any spots have worn red, they may be touched up with common black ink, not the writing fluids which are greenish at first, for they contain nitric acid. A five-cent bottle of ink will go a long way in blackening a harness, and it is cheaper to use it than to make blacking for one harness alone. When the ink or blacking is dry, every strap should be oiled, and after lying until the next day, rubbed dry. Lamp-black or other pigment should never be mixed with the oil, to rub off and smut everything that touches it. A French *cirage* for harness is made as follows : Melt one pound of beeswax ; add two ounces of litharge, and stir until thoroughly incorporated ; let the mixture partly cool, and add three ounces of fine ivory black ; heat up again until it boils, stirring continuously. When nearly cool, add spirits of turpentine, to form a stiff paste. After the harness is thoroughly cleaned, blackened and oiled, it is given a dressing of this *cirage*, and rubbed with a soft shoe-brush until it shines.

A fly-net is a very necessary part of an outfit for driving in fly-time. It protects the horse from much suffering and annoyance, and thereby contributes greatly to the driver's peace of mind.

CARRIAGES AND OTHER VEHICLES.

From the " one-hoss shay " of our grandfathers to the luxurious vehicles of to-day is a long step. American road-wagons and other light rigs are the best in the world. An attempt to describe or even enumerate the various styles of carriages, buggies, wagons and road-carts, which bear witness to the skill of American wheel-wrights, would be vain. Most of the large establishments issue catalogues, which are furnished free on application. There are also smaller shops in nearly every town, which turn out good work, and rural dwellers generally find it advisable to patronize some near-by establishment, rather than buy from a distant and unknown maker. Whatever the style of the vehicle—whether it is a light cart, a capacious family carry-all, or anything between—good material and conscientious workmanship are much the cheapest in the end. Putty, paint and varnish may be made to cover a multitude of sins ; and a flimsy, showy concern, which begins to call for repairs about as soon as the first gloss is off, is dear at any price.

The carriage should be kept in some place far enough from the stable to escape its emanations. Ammoniacal gases arising from a stable or manure heap will rapidly destroy the brilliancy of the best varnish. When first brought home, the carriage should be washed in cold soft water at least three times, to harden the varnish, before it is used. Hose should never be employed for this purpose, a soft sponge, free from grit, and a watering-pot being the proper means for applying water. Neither soap nor warm water should be used under any circumstances, as they are destructive to varnish. If possible, all mud and dirt should be removed before the carriage is put away after it is used, and none ever permitted to dry on. Clean cold water is to be sprinkled on without rubbing, until all dirt runs off with the water, and then the carriage is thoroughly dried with a chamois skin wrung out of clean cold water.

The spindles must be kept well oiled at all times, or the friction will soon cut them and the boxes. As a lubricant for light carriages nothing is better than castor-oil. The wheel is most conveniently lifted from the ground by the lever of a wagon-jack placed under the axle. There is an infinite variety of forms for this implement,

Fig. 63.—REVERSIBLE WAGON-JACK.

one of which is illustrated in figure 63. Its construction is so clearly seen that no description is necessary. The wheel being taken off, the spindle and box are wiped with a clean rag. If any gum has accumulated, it may first be removed by kerosene, which is afterwards wiped off. Then only as much castor-oil is applied to the spindle as will remain on the upper part without running off. The wheel and nut are then replaced, and the others treated in the same way. Good leather washers should be kept on the axles at the collar and nut, and renewed as often as necessary, to keep dirt out of the box. Some hubs are fitted with metallic caps to protect the inside.

All nuts and bolts should be tried frequently with a wrench, to see that none are loose.

A covering of cotton cloth, large enough to envelope the entire vehicle from the hubs upward, should be kept on at all times when the carriage is not in use.

A coat of varnish, once every six months, will keep the carriage bright, and save re-painting for several years.

CHAPTER IX.

THE HORSE'S FOOT; SHOEING AND CARE.

THE foot is one of the most highly organized parts of the horse's anatomy. It is a combination of bones, cartilages, tendons, nerves, and blood vessels, enclosed in skin, hair and tough, elastic envelope. The hoof is a horny crust, very dense on the outer surface, while the interior is made up of thin plates or laminæ, by which it is attached to the coffin-bone. The ground surface of the foot is shown in figure 64. It consists of the sole, the bars and the frog. These protect the sensitive portions of the foot from external injuries. The frog occupies the posterior part of the foot, the insensitive or horny frog containing a deep cleft. On either side of the frog, between it and the sole, are similar clefts, called commissures, the outer sides of which are called the bars, the entire substance being continuous with the horny sole and hoof. This corrugated structure enables the

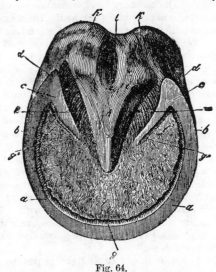

Fig. 64.

GROUND SURFACE OF HORSE'S FORE FOOT.

a, a, outer wall or crust ; *a, b, c,* quarters ; *d, d,* angle of bars ; *e, m,* commissures ; *f, f, f,* sole ; *g,* white line ; *h,* frog ; *i, i,* points of frog ; *k, k,* bulbs of frog , *l,* cleft of frog.

posterior portion of the foot to expand at every step. At the same time the elastic laminæ and horny sole allow the coffin-bone, bearing the weight of the horse, to spring downward, breaking the force of the concussion which would ensue if the foot were a solid, non-elastic mass. The force of the impact is also modified by the plantar cushion, which is interposed between the horny frog and bars and the navicular joint.

In the fore feet the hoof is thickest in the anterior portion, but in the hind feet, the greatest thickness of horn is in the quarters and posterior part. This difference admirably adapts all the feet to their respective requirements.

A sectional view of the foot, with the lower part of the cannon bone, is given in figure 65. Of the three large bones, which are analogous to those of a human finger or toe, the lower or coffin-bone, is enclosed by the hoof. It is of open, porous structure, permeated with nerves and blood vessels. The great plantar artery, with its numerous ramifications, supplies the foot with arterial blood. The coronary band, *k*, contains one of these branches, which maintains the growth of the hoof. The sesamoid and navicular bones act as pulleys, over which play the tendons that move the foot.

When the horse is in its original wild and free condition, the growth of the hoofs keeps even pace with their wear. But in the domesticated condition, with labor upon hard and stony roads, the wear exceeds the growth, and the necessity arises for protecting the hoof by an iron or steel rim around its outer edge. It is plainly evident that the nearer this can be made to conform to the natural conditions and functions of the foot, the better. Yet there seems to be an unfortunate lack of correct ideas concerning the true principles of horse-shoeing.

William Russell, after an experience of more than forty years as a practical horse-shoer, writes: " If we wish to examine a perfect foot, as nature made it, it is generally necessary to find one that has never been shod, for the common mode of shoeing is so frequently destructive, that we seldom meet with a horse that has not lost in some degree the original form, and this deviation from the natural shape is generally proportioned to the length of time it has worn shoes."

The shoe should be as light as possible to withstand the wear and perform the service required. The coffin-bone of the foot is open and porous in its texture, to impart lightness to the foot, yet the design of nature is defeated by loading the feet with too heavy shoes. In the young animal, shod for the first time, we have the appearances presented by a perfectly normal foot, which requires no preparation whatever for the proper application of the shoe, beyond slightly levelling with the rasp the ground surface of the outer crust. After a horse has once been shod, the excess of horn which is to be removed exists at the toe. The wear at this point is prevented by the firm nailing of the shoe, and the consequent absence of all attrition, while at the heels, constant friction goes on between the two opposing surfaces, and modifies the growth. Any excess of

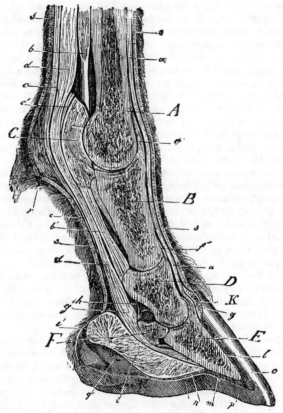

Fig. 65.—SECTION OF HORSE'S FOOT.

A, Cannon bone; *B*, Large pastern; *C*, Sesamoid bone; *D*, Small pastern or coronary bone; *E*, Coffin bone; *F*, Navicular bone; *a, a*, Extensor tendon of the foot; *b, b*, Superior sesamoidal ligament; *c, c*, Flexor perforatus; *d, d*, Flexor perforans; *e, f* and *g*, Capsular ligaments of joints; *h*, Navicular joint; *i*, Fatty frog or plantar cushion; *k*, Coronary band; *l*, Laminæ; *m, n*, Sensitive sole; *o*, White line; *p*, Horny sole; *q*, Sensitive frog; *r*, Fetlock; *e*, Skin of the leg.

growth at the toe renders the pasterns more oblique, and as a consequence throws undue weight upon the back sinews, while too
great height of heels has a similar effect upon the joints of the extremities, by rendering them too upright. The front of the hoof in a
normal condition is at an angle of about 50 degrees with the ground
surface. Taking as our guide the foot of the animal that has never
been brought to the forge, and which in consequence, must be considered as a correct model, let the external wall of the hoof be
reduced nearly to a level with the firm unpared sole. The sole requires no reduction whatever, and should be left untouched. Nature
provides, by a process of exfoliation, for any excess of growth.
Those who advocate the removal and paring out of the sole for the
purpose of giving a supposed elasticity to this part, forget that, by
so doing, they take away the natural defence against injury and
disease for which no substitute can be employed. The frog is also
to be retained in its full integrity, requiring neither paring nor cutting, beyond trimming off the ragged masses. The almost universal
custom of destroying the natural buttresses which exist at the posterior portions of the foot by cutting deep notches in them is as
irrational as it is barbarous. No process could be devised which
would lead more speedily or surely to the contraction and consequent destruction of all the tissues of this region, than this "opening
up of the heels." No man has ever yet been met with who could
offer a satisfactory reason for this mutilation of the foot. Rasping
the crust of the hoof should never be allowed. The removal of the
external horny fibres exposes those beneath to atmospheric influ-
ences. They are not fitted for such exposure, whereby the crust
is weakened, rendered brittle, and liable to crack. Moreover, this
process of rasping removes the natural external polish which gives
such a beautiful surface to the healthy foot, and which no substitute in the form of oil or blacking can supply. The very existence
of such a polish or varnish is ignored by many farriers, who merci-
lessly rasp the entire wall, and think to conceal their ignorance by
giving it a coat of some so-called "hoof ointment."

There are faults in the shoe most commonly employed, which
had their origin in its particular adaptation to the foot after this had
undergone more or less mutilation at the hands of the farrier, and
which have been retained more through custom than actual necessity. In a state of nature we know that every portion of the foot
comes to the ground, and sustains its share of weight, and in the
shod state it should do the same as far as practicable. The shoe
should be beveled upon the ground surface in imitation of the concavity of the sole. If the sole has been left without interference,

little beveling is needed on the upper surface of the shoe, where the space thus formed serves as a lodging place for small stones and other foreign bodies. In shape it should follow the exact outline of the outer wall, being narrow at the heels, but continued of the same thickness throughout. Lateral projections at the quarters, and posterior ones at the heels are unsightly, and should never be allowed. One of the highest authorities says on this point: "In fitting the shoe to the back part of the foot, let the smith take care that it is not longer or wider than the point where the crust and bars unite. An eighth of an inch may be allowed to project backward beyond this point, and not more, but there should not be the slightest over-lapping sideways." In fine, the shoe should be accurately fitted to the foot as previously prepared, and not the foot to the shoe.

The use of calkins has its objections, but as yet no other contrivances have answered the same purpose as well. They should never be employed, however, except when absolutely required, and then they should be of equal length at toe and heels, otherwise an unequal strain is thrown upon tendons and ligaments, terminating sooner or later in serious injury to the extremities. Clips are useful as a means of fastening the shoe more securely, and of diminishing the number of nails. They are particularly desirable on heavy draft horses employed on paved streets. But the toe must be cut out as little as possible for the clip, and the latter must never be hammered back into the hoof. A nail should never be driven in the same part of a shoe where there is a clip. The shoe should not be applied hot to the foot and held there until it is burned into place. But it may safely be touched momentarily to the hoof to mark the points which need removal.

The number and situation of the nails are points of great importance, the determination of which depends upon the kind of work expected of the horse. For light work five in each forward shoe and seven in each hind one have proved amply sufficient. Draft horses will need more. Nails are to be driven in the toe and outside quarter, leaving the heel free to expand. When it is remembered that the introduction of every nail is so much injury to the structures of the foot, it will readily be seen that the smaller the number requisite for the purpose, the better for the animal. In driving the nails, it is essential that a thick, short hold of the crust should be had, rather than a long thin one. The points of the nails should be shortened to just that length which will permit them to be turned over and hammered down smoothly, with the least possible rasping. The common method of rasping notches for the extremities of the nails is not advisable. In fact, the rasp should never be used upon the external walls of the hoof, except in cases of absolute necessity to prevent striking the opposite limb.

In the prairie regions and the great plateaus beyond the Missis-

Fig. 66.—TIP.

sippi shoes are dispensed with to a considerable extent. In all rural districts where the soil is sandy and free from gravel, there is less need of shoes, at least on horses employed in farm work, than is generally conceded. In many situations, however, the hoof, if wholly unprotected, would wear away faster than the growth would make up, yet a full shoe is unnecessary. A tip or segment just large enough to protect the toe, shown in figure 66, is sufficient. This leaves the frog and all the posterior portion of the foot in their normal condition.

Clear and simple as are the principles upon which horse-shoeing is founded, there seems to be much misapprehension regarding them. Patents have been obtained upon great massive shoes, with taps into which calkins are to be screwed as one set after another wears out, the idea being that the shoe should remain without resetting. Such contrivances show total inattention to the physiology of the horse's foot, and the constant growth of the hoof is left wholly out of consideration. A writer in the *Mark Lane Express* summarizes the matter as follows :

"*Defects in Shoeing.*—1. Fitting the shoe too hot, so as to burn and dry the horn. 2. Applying short shoes so that a deep slit must be cut at the toe to let the shoe back. 3. Hammering a shoe into its place without drawing the nails, after it has shifted when nailing it on. 4. Nails' heads projecting above the shoe. 5. Clinches being unlevel or rasped off. 6. Rasping the front of the hoof. 7. The shoes are usually too heavy. 8. Shoes are allowed to remain on too long. 9. Shoes either too short or too long. 10. Shoes not having a level bearing for foot to stand upon. 12. Shoes bolder on the ground surface outer edge than on the foot surface outer edge. 13. Nail holes put too far back. 14. Too large nails being used. 15. Drawing the heel nails up first, or all on one side of the foot before any on the other. 16. The calkin or wedge of one heel being higher than the other. 17. A space being left between the shoe and foot at the heel, 'springing' or 'easing the heel' as it is termed.

"*Good Points in Shoeing.*—1. An even level surface for both bearing surface of foot and shoe, no calkins or wedges being present. 2. The shoe should be same width, length and shape of the foot. 3. The wall and bars only of the foot should be leveled with the rasp. The frog and sole should be left untouched. 4. The shoe should be as light as possible to last a month's wear. 5. Clinches should be level with each other, and not rasped away. 6. The nails should not extend farther back than about three-fourths of the distance from toe to heel on the outer side of foot, and not more than four-fifths on the inner, and the heads should not project beyond the surface of the shoes. 7. The clips should be small."

SHOEING DEFECTIVE FEET.

INTERFERING is striking the inside of the pastern or above it with the shoe of the opposite foot. It is generally caused by toeing in or out, or by such defective formations of the foot, as are illustrated in figures 20 and 23. Various forms of shoes have been devised to correct the evil, the inner quarter being narrower and thicker than the outside. The inside quarter of the hoof is pared enough more than the outside to equalize the difference in the thickness of the two sides of the shoe. It is then nailed on like any other.

PUMICE FOOT is one of the sequelæ of acute laminitis or founder, of which more is said in the next chapter. The hoof becomes light, soft and spongy, the sole loses its elasticity and concave form, and sinks down under the pressure of the coffin - bone. For this evil and some forms of navicular disease, the following device has proved beneficial: Plates, shaped as shown in figure 67, are cut

Fig. 67.—PLATE.

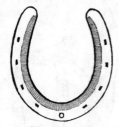

Fig. 68.—SHOE.

from an old saw-blade, the temper having first been drawn. A small tongue of metal is left at the toe and a hole is punched in it. The edge of each plate is heated and struck into the beveled upper surface of the shoe, giving it a slight concavity downward. The shoe is perforated with a rivet-hole at the toe, as shown in figure 68. The foot is nicely leveled, the frog, sole and bars being left untouched, and the shoe fitted to it. The plate is then retempered and riveted to the shoe, the toe of the hoof is rasped to make a seat for the tongue of the plate. The shoe is applied and the two forward nails lightly driven, a cushion of tarred oakum is laid in, and the nailing completed. Finally, as much more oakum as can be crowded in at the heel is shoved under the plate, care being used not to let it lie in lumps, but to make a firm, even cushion, bearing equally on sole and frog. The shod foot is illustrated in figure 69.

OVERREACHING is striking the heel of the fore foot by the hind one when traveling rapidly. The trouble is caused by lack of promptness in picking up the fore feet. The usual method of shoeing to guard against this is to shorten the toes of the hind shoes. This is not always an effective preventive, for it is not the toe but the under edge of the hind shoe that does the mischief. The more recent method is to shorten the toes of the forward shoes, and make them as light as possible, and make the hind shoes heavy at the toes, so that the horse will pick up his fore feet in time to get them out of the way of the hind ones.

CORNS are bruises of the sensitive sole in the inside quarter of one or both fore feet. The primary cause is shoeing in such a manner as to keep the frog from touching the ground. It is not easy to

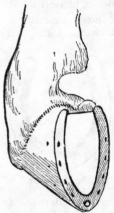

detect their presence, though lameness ensues in bad or neglected cases. But if the horse goes lame when trotting on a hard road, stands uneasily upon his fore feet, and tries to bear his weight upon their outer side, corns may be suspected. The shoes should be removed, and the sole in the angle between the inner quarter and the bars of the lame feet pared. If there are corns, an inflamed appearance will be found, the horn soft and spongy, and in bad cases suppuration. All morbid substance is to be cut out, leaving the bars and frog untouched. The following dressing may be applied: Melt together four ounces each of beeswax and tar, add six ounces of glycerine and two drachms of nitric acid, and stir till cold.

Fig. 69.—THE FOOT SHOD.

The feet must be shod in a manner to give the frog its natural action. The old method is to put on bar shoes, which give temporary relief, as the frog rests upon the bars. But it is much better to shoe the horse so that the frog can touch the ground at every step. If it is not to be driven on hard pavements, tips are sufficient; otherwise shoes must be used which are light and without calkins.

SAND CRACK is a fissure in the horny wall, extending from the coronet to the lower edge. In severe or long-continued cases the opening extends to the sensitive laminæ with inflammation and swelling of the coronal band. In the fore feet it generally affects the inside quarters, and in the hind feet the toes. It is generally caused by improper shoeing, rasping the outside of the hoof, paring the sole, and burning the horn with hot shoes. If there is much soreness, the foot had better be poulticed with flaxseed or soaked in tepid water. Sand, dirt or other foreign substances that have entered the crack must be removed. Various methods of treatment are practiced. One is "cross-firing," which consists of drawing a red hot iron on the hoof transversely across both sides of the crack, about half an inch below the coronet. Another method is to draw one line with the firing iron obliquely downward on each side of the fissure, making a V with the point at the crack. Binding or riveting the fissure is used with or without firing. The two sides are brought together by means of wire or strong cord passed through holes bored for the purpose in the hoof, care being used not to make them so deep as to press upon the sensitive parts. If the crack is in the toe, a small notch is cut in the edge of the hoof at the bottom of the crack, to take all pressure from the shoe at that point. The shoe has a small clip at either side of the crack to prevent expansion. If toe calkins are used, they are set well back from the toe of the shoe. In case of quarter crack, a groove is cut in the lower edge of the hoof, as for toe crack, and a bar shoe applied.

DAILY CARE OF THE FEET.

When the horse returns to the stable from a drive, one of the first duties is to clean and pick out the feet, and examine them to see if any stones have lodged above the shoe, or sharp-pointed object has penetrated the sole. The hind feet should never be allowed to stand in an acrid mass of filth and droppings. Neglect in this particular is a prolific source of thrush and other diseases of the foot. The old and almost universal practice of "stopping" the fore feet with cow-dung, either alone or mixed with clay, is a pernicious one. The very books which recommend this practice also cite it as one of the most usual causes of thrush and canker. If the sole and frog are left as they should be, without interference, there will be less tendency to contraction of the feet. If the fore feet become dry and feverish from stabling upon a plank floor, or traveling on hard roads, they may be soaked in the foot-bath described on page 62. There are also "water-boots" and pads to be used for soaking the feet. "Hoof ointments" and nostrums of all kinds are worse than useless on feet which are properly shod and managed.

CHAPTER X.

AILMENTS AND THEIR REMEDIES.

IT is not the intention of this little work to make an amateur horse-doctor of every person who has the care of a horse. Veterinary science has attained as high a development as any other branch of medical science, and a thorough knowledge of it can be acquired only by long study and experience. No department of science has been marked by greater reforms than veterinary practice. The old barbarous methods of indiscriminate bleeding, blistering, purging, firing, and other "heroic" treatment, have been superseded by an enlightened system, which is indicated as follows by the writings of two eminent veterinary authorities. Dr. Dixon says: "Nature is ever busy, by the silent operation of her own forces, in curing disease. Her medicines are air, warmth, food, water, and sleep." Again: "Blood is the fuel that keeps the lamp of life burning; if the fuel be withdrawn, the vital spark is extinguished." Dr. Geo. H. Dadd says in his "Modern Horse Doctor": "During nine years' practice in the city of Boston, the author of this work has never in a single case of any form of disease had recourse to the practice of blood-letting." Similar citations could be multiplied, all showing a thorough reform in veterinary practice. Cathartics, diuretics or surgical interference of any kind should never be resorted to by any one but a qualified practitioner. In fact, if a horse worth saving is attacked with any serious ailment, the only safe course is to call a veterinary surgeon, if one can be obtained.

Yet there are some ills which horse-flesh is heir to, so sudden and violent in their development, and fatal in their results, that all horse-keepers should know something of their pathology and symptoms, as well as the means of rendering at least the first aid, or the horse may die before professional assistance can arrive. There are other, less acute affections, which call for care and good management rather than medical or surgical treatment. In every case prevention is better than cure, and to secure this the horse-keeper should have some knowledge of morbid conditions and their causes. We shall briefly mention a few ailments which are most likely to require attention.

ACUTE DISEASES OF THE BOWELS.

SPASMODIC COLIC is violent and rapid. The attack usually comes without the slightest warning. The horse paws violently, kicks at his belly, puts his nose to his flanks, lies down, rolls on his back, breathing heavily. The paroxysm seems to cease, the horse rises, shakes himself and looks for food, but there is a sudden recurrence of the spasms, the sufferer breaks into profuse perspiration, and throws himself about as before. In an hour or two either the intervals between the spasms are longer, or they become more and more violent and death ensues. Many of the more evident symptoms of colic resemble those which indicate inflammation of the bowels, while the pathology and treatment of the two diseases are quite unlike. Youatt points out in the following table the means of determining one from the other.

COLIC.	INFLAMMATION OF THE BOWELS.
Sudden in its attack, and without any warning.	Gradual in its approach, with previous indications of fever.
Pulse rarely much quickened in the early period of the disease, and during the intervals of ease, but evidently fuller.	Pulse very much quickened, but small and often scarcely to be felt.
Legs and ears of natural temperature.	Legs and ears cold.
Relief obtained from rubbing the belly.	Belly exceedingly painful, and tender to the touch.
Relief obtained from motion.	Pain evidently increased by motion.
Intervals of rest and ease.	Constant pain.
Strength scarcely affected.	Great and evident weakness.

The causes of colic are improper feeding, either in quality or quantity; drinking to excess of cold water, or standing unprotected in the cold air, when heated. The horse should be placed at once in a roomy box stall, well littered down with straw. At the first quiet interval between spasms the following may be given as a drench: Chloroform, tincture of opium, sulphuric ether, each one ounce ; linseed oil eight ounces. This is one dose. Or the following : Tincture of opium, tincture of capsicum, essence of peppermint, tincture of rhubarb, spirits of camphor, each one half ounce ; to be mixed in half a pint of molasses and one pint of water. Divide into two equal doses, to be given at an interval of half an hour. Injections may also be given of aloes dissolved in warm water. The operation of these remedies is aided by walking the horse around, and rubbing the belly with a brush or hot flannel cloth. After an attack of colic a horse should be given several days of rest, for even if apparently cured, he will be sore and weak all through.

FLATULENT COLIC is not as violent or rapid in its course as the preceding. It is generally caused by gorging with green food. The horse paws the ground or its stall, hangs its head and has a dull, sleepy aspect. Then there is a visible distention of the belly and great uneasiness. The symptoms may continue several days before recovery or death. The treatment should be of a character to move the bowels and relieve them of the pressure. Mix two ounces of aromatic spirits of ammonia in half a pint of linseed oil, and administer as a drench. The lower bowels are impacted and must be relieved by back-raking. The hand, well oiled, is carefully intro-duced up the rectum, and its contents withdrawn. Then an injec-tion is given of warm water and castile soap. If the animal is not relieved, take one ounce hyposulphite of soda, one ounce pulverized charcoal, dissolve and mix in one pint of water, and horn it down the animal's throat. If the case is a protracted one, this may be alternated after an interval of a few hours with a dose consisting of one-fourth ounce chloride of lime in half a pint of linseed oil. We do not recommend any attempt to puncture the bowels with a view of liberating the gas. If performed successfully, it must be done by a skilled operator.

INFLAMMATION OF THE BOWELS is often the sequel of colic. It is also caused by sudden chills, external violence, etc. The symp-toms are described above. As the disease develops, however, there are signs which clearly distinguish one from the other, for in inflam-mation of the bowels there is no cessation from violent pain, and the pulse is increasingly full, firm and rapid ; no appetite ; labored breathing, distressed and anxious countenance, pawing, lying down and rising, etc. The treatment consists of mild laxatives with anodynes in infusion of slippery elm bark, with external fomenta-tions. Don't bleed. Dr. Geo. H. Dadd, after citing the recom-mendations of copious bleeding, remarks : " Let the reader omit the blood-letting, and have recourse, if the nature of the case requires it, to a drench and injection, together with such other restorative means as we shall recommend, and there will be no need of abstract-ing blood." " The indications of cure in inflammation of the bowels is to equalize the circulation and remove irritation and obstructions to vital action." " Purgatives cannot always be given with safety in inflammation of the bowels, because they might tend to augment the previous irritability of the alimentary canal. A dose of cathar-tic medicine may, however, be mixed with lubricants, for example, slippery elm, mucilage of gum arabic, or olive oil, so as to defend the sensitive parts, and at the same time not deprive the medicine of its cathartic properties." The following remedies are recommended, each being one dose : (1) Linseed oil, 8 ounces ; lime water, 2 ounces. Or (2) Epsom salts, 8 ounces ; thin gruel, 1 quart. Or (3) Pulverized aloes, 4 drachms ; mucilage of slippery elm, 1 pint. Or (4) Common salt, 6 ounces ; warm water 1 pint. The last (4) is also administered in the form of frequent injections, but fatal superpurgation must be guarded against. External applications are made to the belly, of flannel bandages wrung out of hot water. Dry sheets are bound over these to check evaporation. An infusion of hops is given when great pain is manifested. To make this, pour a quart of hot water over two ounces of hops, let it stand until cool, then strain and sweeten with honey.

THE MOUTH AND TEETH.

There is more suffering by horses from deformed, irregular and carious teeth than is generally suspected. Misshapen or irregular teeth interfere with mastication, and lead to loss of condition, and even more serious results. One or more of the front teeth sometimes become broken or loosened. In the latter case there should be prompt removal. The grinders sometimes grow irregularly, lacerating the tongue or cheek, and the horse unable to masticate its food, rolls it around in the mouth, and rejects it. This is called "quidding." The teeth should be carefully examined and all irregularities removed by a tooth-rasp. The so called "wolf-teeth" or "buck-teeth," about which there are so many superstitious notions, are simply supernumerary teeth, which should be removed carefully with forceps, and not cruelly knocked out with hammer and chisel, at the great risk of breaking the jaw. Decayed teeth are the often unsuspected cause of much suffering and poor condition. A horse with a carious molar feels the pangs of toothache as keenly as a human being can. An unsound tooth gradually breaks away and the opposing sound tooth grows rapidly to fill the vacancy. The first should be promptly removed by forceps made for the purpose, and the second cut down to its normal size. Horse dentistry has become an important profession in the larger cities, and its practice requires skill and experience. Every horse-keeper should know enough about his horse's teeth to detect the need of professional interference. But avoid quack "hoss dentists."

"LAMPAS."—Horses are subject during dentition, and from other causes, to swelling and inflammation in the lining membrane of the mouth. The suffering animal gets off his feed, and the ignorant attendant pronounces it a case of "lampas." Some village "horse doctor" or blacksmith is called in to operate, or the owner may do it himself. The inflamed and sensitive membranes are scarified by knives or seared with hot irons, to remove the supposed disease. The symptoms need not cause any uneasiness, nor do they call for heroic treatment. Soft food should be given, with an occasional

Fig. 70.—MUZZLE FOR CRIBBER.

bran mash, and if the appetite is affected, a dose of mild laxative medicine may be administered, and the mouth washed out with a solution of chlorate of potash, or a wash composed of half a fluid ounce of chloralum, and one ounce tincture of myrrh in half a pint of water. If the bars are greatly inflamed, slight scarification with a lancet may be necessary, and if a grinder is coming with excessive tumefaction of the gum, a cross-cut directly over the tooth will be beneficial.

CRIBBING is not a disease, but is both the consequence and the cause of a morbid condition of the stomach. The horse rests its upper front teeth upon the edge of the manger or any fixed object, stretches its neck and belches air with a peculiar grunting noise. Addiction to the habit can readily be detected by the worn and rounded appearance of the upper cutting teeth. It may be prevented by the use of the muzzle halter illustrated in figure 70. At the same time it is well to give the horse chalk or ashes with its food, or sprinkle it with magnesia, to correct the acidity of the stomach.

PARASITES.

MANGE is a troublesome evil, nearly analogous to itch in human beings. It is caused by small mites or *acari*, which burrow under the cuticle and cause intense itching with tumefaction and loss of hair. The most effective remedy is Thymo-cresol, a preparation which has recently come into use as an insecticide and anti-parasite on all kinds of live stock.

RAT'S TAIL is the rather significant name for a cutaneous affection of the dock, which causes the hair of the tail to fall out. Whether caused by parasites or not, the same remedy is effectively used for this as for mange.

LICE are often communicated to horses from hen-roosts, which are allowed near the stable. The hens and their roosts should be removed, and the entire premises given a coat of hot whitewash of lime and carbolic acid. The Thymo-cresol may then be applied.

BOTS are the larvæ of a gad-fly, which deposits its eggs upon the hair of the legs, sides and shoulders, from which they are licked by the horse's tongue, and carried into the stomach in the act of swallowing. The larvæ, which hatch from the eggs, attach them-

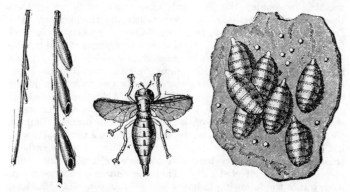

Fig. 71.—EGGS. Fig. 72.—FEMALE FLY. Fig. 73.—BOTS IN HORSE'S STOMACH.

selves to the lining membrane of the stomach, and remain there until the following spring. They then become detached, pass through the alimentary canal and fall with the droppings. They become pupæ and enter the ground, where they remain until the final transformation, when they emerge as flies. Figure 71 shows the eggs of natural size and magnified; figure 72 the fly of natural size; figure 73 a portion of the lining membranes of the stomach with the bots adhering.

No means of expelling bots has ever been found. They have been known to live for days in solutions of arsenic and other active poisons. There is no known substance which will expel them without killing the horse. It is generally agreed by all who have studied the subjects that these parasites are not injurious to the health of the horse, unless they are in such numbers as to interfere with digestion. In fact, some writers hold that their presence is in some unknown way beneficial. The eggs can be removed from the hair by rubbing with a sponge or coarse cloth wrung out of hot water.

SCRATCHES, OR GREASE.

Exposure of the feet and legs to melting snow or mud, with neglect to clean them, standing in a filthy or underground stable, and any cause which interferes with the circulation, and leaves the legs in an unclean condition, produce scratches or grease, the symptoms of which are unfortunately too well known to need description. The first steps in any treatment is perfect cleanliness, washing or soaking the feet and legs in soft warm water, then thoroughly drying them. If taken when the inflammation and cracking of the skin first appear, the following application is beneficial: Rose water, 8 ounces; glycerine, 8 ounces; sugar of lead in solution, 1 ounce. If the disease becomes so far developed that deposits have formed on the heels with fungus growths, constitutional treatment is necessary. Dr. Dadd recommends the following, if the horse is in good condition : Powdered aloes, 4 drachms ; powdered gentian, 2 drachms ; ginger, 1 drachm ; mixed in a pint of warm water, and sweetened with molasses. Give as a drench. Make a poultice of pulverized slippery elm bark, mixed to a thick paste with hot water, spread on thick cloth, add a sprinkling of dilute carbolic acid, powdered bayberry bark and powdered charcoal, and when cool apply to the affected parts. This may remain on for one night. Afterwards the following liniment will be found useful : Vaseline, 12 ounces ; barbadoes tar, 6 ounces ; spirits of turpentine, 4 ounces; oil origanum, 6 ounces ; verdigris, half an ounce. Apply once daily, shaking well before using. Feed no corn, little if any oats, but give green food, carrots, apples, and frequent bran mashes.

ACUTE LAMINITIS, OR FOUNDER.

Acute inflammation of the feet is caused by rapid driving on hard, dry roads or heated pavements, drinking freely of hard cold water when the body is heated by exercise, gorging with grain or any rich food, and sometimes by sympathetic affection with inflammation of the lungs or other parts of the system. It generally attacks the fore feet, but may affect all. The first symptoms are difficulty in the gait, the affected animal stepping as if trying to walk on its heels. There is every expression of extreme pain, the eyes glare, the nostrils are distended, and there is a trembling all over. If examined the feet will be found too hot, with the artery in the pastern throbbing violently. The first step towards relief is to remove the shoes as gently as possible, and wash the feet in warm water. Then fasten a large flat sponge under each foot, and wrap the feet and legs from the sole upward with flannel bandages, and keep them wet with dilute tincture of arnica, half a pint of the tincture to a gallon of water. Give fifteen to twenty drops (according to the size of the horse) of tincture of aconite root, and two ounces of saltpetre in a pint of warm water, to be repeated twice at intervals of twelve hours, the doses to be diminished at each repetition. Feed nothing but bran mashes, boiled carrots, and other soft food. The bandages are to be kept moistened for several days, until the violence of the symptoms subside.

GLANDERS AND FARCY.

GLANDERS is a malignant and incurable disease. It is spontaneous only with the horse species, but is also contagious, and when communicated to the human species, produces terrible suffering and death. In its acute form its development is so rapid and the symptoms are so clearly marked, that there is little difficulty in recognizing it, and taking summary measures to prevent its spread. In the chronic form it may exist for months, communicating its virus to healthy animals before its presence is positively known. Foul stables, exposure, excessive labor, neglect and bad management may produce glanders and farcy. Says Dr. Dadd: "Suppose we select a horse whose general health is impaired; let such animal be exposed to the pitiless storm for several hours, and he will take what is termed in popular language a 'cold.' Let him now be treated according to the practice of the 'kill or cure' system—*bleeding* and *purging*. The secretions become impaired; loss of appetite sets in; the 'coat stares'; there is a dull, sleepy appearance about the animal, and a discharge from the nostrils, at first thin and opaque, but which soon acquires a tenacious and acrimonious character; it finally assumes a putrid type and decomposes parts of the mucous surfaces; ulcerations of the cartilages of the nose follow, and we have a clear case of glanders." The symptoms of acute glanders are fever, dull and heavy countenance, discharge from one or both nostrils, at first thin and watery, and afterward purulent, the glands under the jaws are swollen, tumid and adhering to the jaw bone. The nostrils sometimes become swollen and stick together by the discharge, and a fetid odor is emitted. If the nostrils are opened, ulcers may be found in them. Blood poisoning, stupor and death ensue. In the chronic form there is discharge and ulceration of the nostrils, but little fever; the appetite becomes capricious, there is a general wasting of the body, and the animal dies. Upon the appearance of any of the symptoms described above, the best course to pursue is to isolate the animal beyond chance of contact with others, and call a skilled veterinarian and place the case in his hands. There are other complaints which have some of the incipient symptoms of glanders, and many horses are doubtless sacrificed through mistaking them for the loathsome disease.

FARCY is the milder form of disease which often runs into glanders. The characteristic symptoms of farcy are dullness, lack of appetite, and in some cases swollen legs. Corded swellings appear on the neck, inside the legs and in other parts. In time these become inflamed, small, suppurative tumors arise upon them and burst, discharging an ichorous fluid. These are called farcy buds. With skillful treatment by a competent practitioner farcy is sometimes cured, if taken before it merges into glanders. But in every pronounced case of glanders the animal should be destroyed, with all harness and clothing that has come in contact with it, and the stable thoroughly fumigated and disinfected.

PRIZE ESSAYS.

CHAPTER XI.

STABLING, FEED AND CARE.

BY ISAAC H. FICKEL, OHIO.

THE horse, according to tradition and history, is found to have been very early associated with man as a domestic animal. He has been an important factor in bringing the human race to its present state of progress and refinement. Whether in war, commerce, or pleasure, no animal so readily responds to the wants of mankind. The question "How to keep the Family Horse," to obtain the best results ; to provide the proper shelter ; to understand food elements and their proportions ; and the disposal of the manure, are matters of great financial importance to every horse owner.

THE STABLE.

In discussing the various questions connected with the stabling of the horse, it must not be forgotten that we have many climates, and many degrees of aridity and moisture to deal with ; and what would be suitable for one place, would not be adapted to other parts of the country.

There are so many excellent plans for stables, adapted to special localities, that it is not necessary to describe any particular ones. Whatever plan has been adopted, there are, however, certain matters to be considered, necessary to the health and comfort of the animal. Most important is a dry location. The horse is a native of a dry country, and cannot be kept in health in a damp situation. Coughs, colds, and other ailments are the result of damp stables. These interfere with the use of the horse, irrespective of other rea-

(121)

sons, as domestic comfort is greatly dependent on the carriage being always at command. This may be secured in most cases by thorough drainage. Every stable should be kept free from dampness. Hardly less important is it to provide the best means of keeping up a tolerably even temperature in summer and winter, and to furnish sufficient ventilation. The horse requires a constant supply of pure air. Pure air is the source of pure blood and pure blood is the source of health. Too many, in their desire to keep their horses comfortable in cold weather, neglect this important matter. Neither man nor beast can enjoy health while inhaling corruption at every breath. Yet many stables are built with little regard to ventilation. The air in the stable should be constantly changed, without creating a draft upon the horse. The impure air can be carried off by ventilators, which should be placed on the top of every stable. The stable should be well lighted. Light exercises as much influence upon animal as upon vegetable life. Many diseases are much more virulent, and the eye cannot retain its full power if deprived of light.

The stable for the horse should be of good size. The narrow dimensions of many of the stalls are a positive cruelty to horses. They are built too narrow to enable the horse to extend his limbs when he desires. He is compelled, when in a recumbent position, to double his limbs up under him, and his legs are thus kept cramped when they should be completely at rest. Box-stalls permit the animal to choose its position and change it at pleasure. Comfort is essential to health, and it is evident that the animal cannot be comfortable when closely tied in a narrow stall. The stalls should be kept clean, and the floor daily sprinkled with some good absorbent, as gypsum, to absorb the foul odors continually arising. Absorbents are not generally used freely enough about stables. Besides having pure air for the animal to breathe, a stable that is stored full of hay and grain ought always to be well ventilated, and kept clean, that the impurities of the air may not penetrate these. All food should be kept as pure as possible. Cleanliness about the stable is just as important to the health of the horse, as cleanliness about the house is important to the health of the family.

MANURE; ITS STORAGE AND DISPOSAL.

Every thoughtful farmer realizes the importance of saving the manure from all his stock. Yet few give it the care necessary to save it as it should be. The urine is the most valuable part of the excrements of animals (being the main source of nitrogen), yet this is mostly allowed to settle into the soil and be lost. How many of our farmers throw the manure under the eaves of the stable, exposing it to the action of air and water, allowing the water to drain off and the manure to heat, thereby losing the most valuable parts. About all that is left may be regarded as husks—of very little value as a fertilizer. It is these little leaks of the farm which make farming so unprofitable to many persons. The manure and urine of the horse, if properly saved, form the strongest and most durable of dressings for meadows, and especially is it valuable when the feed contains a large proportion of albuminoids. It is estimated that one-half the cost of these foods is returned in the increased value of the manure. To one residing in a city, possessing a small lot, this saving is hardly of less importance than to the farmer, as well-decomposed stable manure forms one of the best dressings for the lawn.

In the storage of manure there are two dangers to contend with. The first is the leaching, or allowing it to become saturated with water, which drains off ; and the second is the loss of the nitrogen by escaping and uniting with hydrogen, forming ammonia, which, being very volatile, is easily carried away. But this gaseous ammonia may be converted into a solid and retained. That is, we can unite it with some other substance that will hold it, and this nitrogen is the most costly element in manure, as it enters into the composition of all kinds of vegetable matter. Upon how to overcome these losses, then, will depend the future value of the manure.

To prevent leaching, it is necessary to have a receptacle for manure so that it cannot become saturated and the water drain off. If there be a manure cellar, this is easily avoided ; but if it has to be stored outside, and exposed to the action of the elements, it is not so easily saved. If stored outside, the receptacle for it should be lower than the surrounding surface, so that the water cannot drain off ; it should be neatly piled in a compact, flattened heap.

The escape of nitrogen may be prevented by using absorbents, such as plaster (gypsum), kainit (which are the best materials that can be used to prevent the loss of ammonia), or, when these are lacking, road dust is particularly valuable. By this means the ammonia will unite with the organic acids, and form soluble but not volatile compounds, thus forming a compound rich in nitrogen, lime, and potash. Where straw is largely grown, it should be provided in abundance for bedding, and with a free use of gypsum or other absorbents, most of the urine will be saved. The manure pile should not be allowed to become dry, but should have a few barrels of water added occasionally, and be frequently stirred with a fork. The manure should be drawn to those fields upon which plants are growing, or soon will have them, to absorb it as it dissolves. Thus by a little care and attention, thousands of dollars will be saved annually to farmers, who are now paying high prices for the identical elements in commercial fertilizers which they are permitting to go to loss in their own barnyards.

FEEDING.

The study of the subject of food elements, and their relation to the animal system, has been greatly neglected. Of late years science has been doing much in this line of work, but there is a great deal to be done yet. Although the animal body is so complex in structure, yet chemistry has divided it in a general way into nitrogenous, non-nitrogenous, and mineral matters. Since these substances are continually being destroyed in the body in forming materials for growth, in generating heat, and in producing force, it is necessary that the animal should receive substances similar to those destroyed, so that these may be assimilated by the tissues and fluids of the body to replace those lost and to enable the vital actions to continue.

The object of feeding is to supply the animal with the various elements which enter into its composition, and since the nitrogenous (albuminoids, or protein) and non-nitrogenous (carbohydrates) substances vary only in narrow limits, and since the rate at which each is destroyed in the body is also fixed, it follows that the food which the animal receives should also contain these nutrients in the right proportion. The food given to an animal may contain all the nutrients named, but it may not contain them in the right proportion to supply the animal organism. Some are rich in albuminoids, while others are composed largely of carbohydrates. Hence, in an economical point of view, we should combine these foods to form a mixture in the right proportion to satisfy the needs of the animal system. A large part of the animal body is composed of albuminoids, and as it is impossible for the animal system to convert carbohydrates into albuminoids, the sole source is from those plants containing the albuminoids. The Germans estimate a pound of digestible albuminoids to cost on an average five times as much as a pound of digestible carbohydrates ; it is readily seen that economy requires the least proportion of the former consistent with perfect nutrition. The quantity of carbohydrates which a horse requires, depends upon the latitude and the season. As carbon and hydrogen are the heat-producing elements, it follows that the colder the climate the greater proportion of carbohydrates is needed. We have mentioned the importance of the albuminoids in animal economy. It is evident, then, that the proportion of albuminoids which the feed contains is an important element in determining its value ; and those foods which contain them in the largest quantity are, other things being equal, the most valuable, as these are the most expensive ingredients to produce.

Relatively to size, the horse has a smaller stomach than any other of our domestic animals. This makes it necessary that he must feed frequently, digest promptly, and have a rich material in a small bulk, thus adapting him especially to perform rapid work. In a state of nature he is under no necessity of eating too much at any one time, but replenishes the stomach lightly and at frequent intervals throughout the day. There is no overloading, nor over-tasking the organ, and no extreme exertion upon a full stomach, which so often takes place in the domesticated condition. Even in domestication, a horse will maintain excellent health on the natural grasses, fresh or made into hay; but when he is placed under the saddle or in harness, and subjected to work, we take him from his natural state, and the same feeding will no longer meet the demands of the system.

In regard to the kinds of feeding-stuffs to be used, it must be apparent that, with the many different climates and surroundings in this extensive country, what would be adapted to one section would not suit in other parts. Yet there are three general points to be considered, in order to develop a more rational and more economical system of feeding. First: How much of each of the essential groups of food constituents is contained in the food? Second: How much of each of these essential food constituents is digestible under existing circumstances, and thus directly available to the animal? Third: How much of the three essential food constituents does the animal require to secure the best results? Tables have been prepared, at great labor and expense, for our benefit. The one given below shows the composition and digestibility of the foods usually given to horses.

	COMPOSITION.			DIGESTIBILITY.		
	Protein.	Fat.	Nitrogen, free extract.	Protein.	Fat.	Nitrogen, free extract.
Pasture grass	3.	.8	13.1	75	66	79
Timothy hay	6.2	1.7	45.8	62	20	56
Oat straw	2.3	1.	26.4	38	30	42
Corn fodder	3.	1.1	37.9			
Oats (grain)	9.8	4.9	58.	87	78	77
Corn (dent)	10.5	4.8	70.2	78	63	94
Wheat bran	14.5	3.5	53.6	70	90	75

By reference to this table, it will be seen that the albuminoids (protein) in the hay and grasses are little more than half the amount present in the same weight of grain. Thus the grain furnishes nearly twice the amount of flesh-forming aliment that is supplied in hay ; from which it follows that by its use we can supply the material necessary for the maintenance of the animal without subjecting the stomach to a great distension with food at any one time. Again, it will be observed that the grains contain about one-half more respiratory food in a given bulk than hay and grass, and not more than one-fourth the amount of indigestible woody fiber, so that in the grains we have a doubly nutritious food with incomparably less superfluous matter, and capable of more prompt and thorough digestion. Thus the stomach is soon cleared, and the animal is fit for use sooner after a meal. Hence, the faster and severer the work which a horse is expected to perform, the sounder and more nutritious should be his food. His oats should be increased and his hay diminished. Then the movements of the body and limbs are not impaired, as when fed on bulky food.

By careful experiments, it has been found a ration containing twelve to thirteen pounds of digestible nutrients, and having a nutritive ratio of one to seven (i. e., one pound of albuminoids to seven of carbohydrates, which includes the fat and nitrogen free extract), is sufficient for a horse weighing twelve hundred pounds, and performing light work, such as a family horse would be expected to do. Of this amount there should be digestible substances:

```
Protein ------------------------------------ 1.8 pounds.
Carbohydrates --------------------------11.2    "
Fat -------------------------------------- .6    "
```

The question, From what sources are we to obtain these? brings us to the consideration of the most common foods of the horse.

PASTURE GRASS.—Though no person should allow the family horse to depend upon grass alone, yet, owing to its being his natural food, he should not be deprived of its use entirely. When kept at work, however, it should not be fed to him, owing to its loosening effects upon the bowels; but when not in use, grass, with a portion of good hay and grain, forms an excellent ration.

TIMOTHY.—This is probably the most valuable of all grasses for hay. It is extensively cultivated, contains a large amount of nutritive matter, and forms one of the best foods for horses, if cut in the bloom, and properly cured.

OAT STRAW, if cut at the proper time, forms a feeding stuff not to be despised. Good straw is most decidedly better than poor hay. Its chief value lies in its non-nitrogenous matter, of which it furnishes a cheap supply, and in combination with feeding stuffs which can supply its deficiency in protein it forms a valuable fodder.

CORN FODDER is extensively used in many parts of the country, and though forming a good substitute for hay, it is not as nutritious as good timothy hay, and from the large amount of stalks, it is not nearly as convenient to feed as hay. However, when grown by the owner, it may be used with advantage during the winter season. Of the grains,

OATS seem to be especially adapted to the horse. All grains have high nutritive values, with but little waste; as a consequence, their digestibility is high, and they contain a large amount of nutriment in a small bulk.

CORN is largely fed to horses, but from its tendency to produce fat, it is not to be recommended as equal to oats. Corn may be fed more freely in winter, because it is an excellent heat supporter, but at other times it should be liberally mixed with oats, or discarded entirely.

WHEAT BRAN, it will be seen from the table of analyses, is rich in protein. That it can be fed with profit to our driving horses occasionally, there can be no doubt. When fed in connection with corn or corn meal, its effects are very soon noticed in the appearance of the animal.

Horses, like man, desire a variety of food, and the system tires of a steady diet. There should be a change of food occasionally. Good timothy hay, cut at the right time and properly cured, and oats, then, are the foods which will furnish the best results, all things considered, whether grown by the owner or purchased. Supply and demand may alter the cost of these, when other foods may be substituted, and their values computed from the table of nutritive values. Cutting and steaming food for stock has many advantages, and certainly pays. Whether it will be profitable where only one horse is kept, is a question which must be left to the judgment of the owner. Feed should be given regularly. The human stomach bears hunger better than that of the horse. He should always be allowed plenty of time to eat.

The stomach is in no condition to receive food immediately after severe exertion. At this time it has not nervous force to digest the food, and often flatulent colic is caused by too hurried feeding. Neither should a horse be used directly after eating, but time should be given it to partially digest its food. Neglect of this often causes staggers. Always feed carefully. No scantiness ; no overfeeding, especially of the albuminoids or grain foods.

Good pure water of moderate temperature is of prime importance. It requires the combustion of tissue to warm water to the temperature of the body. Hence, it is important that the water should not be too cold in winter. Owing to the small size of the horse's stomach, he should not be allowed too much water at any one time, especially when warm or after a feed of grain. The old saying, that "a horse has more sense than a man," and that he will not drink too much, is a great mistake. He will drink too much when heated and the stomach is empty; he will also drink too much when the first heat caused by digestion commences. With a little at a time and often no danger is likely to result.

The use of a certain amount of common salt is necessary in many ways to the animal system. This need is increased since many of our domestic animals are stall-fed.

CARE AND MANAGEMENT.

In many respects the horse's constitution is as tender as a man's. Cold storms exhaust its vitality, and in proportion as this exhaustion takes place, an increased consumption of heat-producing food occurs. Hence, during cold and stormy weather, he should be kept in a comfortable stable. In seasons of extreme heat, the horse needs protection from the direct rays of the sun as much as he needs protection from winter storms. Medical men say that men and horses are the only animals that sweat. They perspire through the skin, the pores of which become opened and enlarged, and it is while in this condition that both are exceedingly liable to be injured by overheating.

We are all somewhat familiar with the care that is given to trotting horses. And what is the object of all this care? The purpose is the preservation of health and perfect condition. It is not necessary to give the family horse as much attention as the trotter receives, but it ought to be sufficient to give the animal good treatment, and to insure its comfort to the utmost practical limit. He should be well groomed, for the curry-comb is to the horse what a bath is to man. The prime importance of grooming him thoroughly rests upon the fact, that his health is essentially dependent upon the cleanliness of his hide. The glands must be kept open to allow the dead matters to be cast out of the body. When allowed to do their work, they throw off more deleterious matter than the lungs or kidneys. The curry-comb should be used lightly, however, as it is a source of pain when used roughly. It should be followed by the brush and cloth, to remove the dust that escapes the comb.

Attention to the care of the feet and legs is of great importance. They require more care than the body, and are more liable to injury. When a horse has been driven during the day, he should not be allowed to spend the night without being cleaned, and his limbs rubbed down. This stimulates the circulation, and opens the pores of the skin.

Kindness with the family horse is of the utmost importance. Always cultivate an acquaintance, and be on social and friendly terms with him. If he is tired and worn out, it is astonishing how these little attentions will encourage and cheer him up. When not in use he should be given a reasonable amount of daily exercise. No animal will do well without exercise. It promotes a good action of the limbs, and assists digestion. The harness should be made to fit, thus avoiding chafes and bruises. In cold weather the lips and tongue of the horse may be made very sore by contact with the frozen bit. The bit should always be warmed before being placed in the horse's mouth. Flies are very annoying to horses, and the use of the net, or some preparation that will keep the flies away, is well repaid.

Horses in a state of nature do not require any protection for the hoof. But, in connection with labor and artificial roads, domestication alters more or less the conditions on which the horse depends for the hoof's integrity as an efficient protection to the lining and extremely sensitive parts it encloses. A horse would not be able to travel long on our artificial roads without some protection to the hoof. The art of shoeing is not practised by as skillful workmen as necessity demands. Shoes allowed to remain on too long are often the source of serious foot diseases.

Care in driving is of the greatest importance. How often do we see an animal driven until wet with perspiration, and dotted with foam, standing without blanket or protection of any kind from the cold northern winds ! When in such condition, he evidently suffers intensely ; besides the danger of contracting diseases from which he will never recover. If any law on our statute book should be more rigidly enforced, it is the one against fast driving. A case of a family horse—a noble animal—has just come to the writer's notice. The animal was taken with kidney disease, caused, the veterinarian said, by overdriving, ending in three days in lockjaw and death. Blankets should always be provided in cold weather, so that the horse will dry without chilling. Protect him from drafts when warm, and either rub down, or let him stand in a stable where cold air cannot strike him.

The family horse is especially worthy of the best of care, for no other domestic animal so readily responds to kind treatment. " A righteous man regardeth the life of his beast."

CHAPTER XII.

HOW TO SELECT A HORSE AND KEEP IT.

BY A. F. COLWELL, RHODE ISLAND.

THE horse best adapted for family use ought certainly be of good weight. A small horse cannot do well the work about an ordinary farm or gentleman's place. To haul wood from the lots in winter, and manure from the barn-cellar in spring, to plow, harrow, etc., in the preparation of land, and to take the "democrat" wagon or carryall, with the family, to the city or along the country roads, requires something more than eight or nine hundred pounds of horse-flesh, however willing the animal may be to do all it can. As near eleven hundred pounds as possible should be the rule, for an animal of that weight will be more satisfactory than one lighter. As for blood, there is none perhaps better for general use than the Morgan. Such horses as Hiram Beers drove, when he carried Dr. Wentworth's family to see Barton Cathcart graduate, could hardly be improved on. The late Henry Ward Beecher knew a good horse and described one well. The one owned by the writer is of Hamble-tonian stock, and is possessed of nearly all the good qualities usually sought for. Of course there are hundreds of horses of native stock in New York, and throughout the Central and Western States, that are almost faultless. The two families above are simply mentioned because they are best known.

Among the good points to be noticed in the selection of the family horse, docility and gentleness must be kept well in front. If the women and children are to share in the use and care of the horse, nothing vicious should be tolerated. If sound and previously well cared for, a horse eight, ten, or even twelve years old, may be bought with no fear of disability on account of old age. Mr. John Russel, who recently delivered a series of lectures in Boston on the care of the horse, said that "old wine, old friends, and old horses"—and by that meaning those from eight to fourteen—"should always be preferred to young ones." The horse does not come to maturity as early as some think, as the record of the trotting horse of America shows. A horse ten years old, that has no defect of body or limb, is practically safe from the ordinary horse diseases. So far as outward appearance, color, etc., are concerned, no general directions can be given; but if the buyer is inexperienced, it is better to go to some reliable dealer, stating what is desired, and the amount of money to be given. An honest horse jockey, in some people's minds, is an anomaly, but many such have been found by the writer.

STABLING.

Having bought the horse, the consideration of a proper place to keep him is the next phase of the subject. The stable should be large and light, situated on the south side of the barn, so that the window, which should always be at the end of the stable—covered with wire netting—may be opened in the warmer weather without fear of a draft of cold air from the north or east, in order that fresh air may be easily obtained, and also that the little sunshine there is during the short winter days may light up the stable. There is, in the minds of good horsemen, no doubt but that small, damp, dark stalls, strongly impregnated with ammonia, as such always are, furnish the producing cause of "pinkeye," and sometimes total blindness, and also lead to complications of throat and lung troubles, for which remedies avail but little as long as these conditions remain. The floor should either be double, with the upper layer of boards set edgewise half an inch apart, or have the planks raised at the front of the stall about two inches, and a line of holes or an open crack at the back, so that the urine will at once run off, and so leave the bedding and floor as dry as possible. In the winter, when the shoes have long sharp calks, they may catch between the cracks in the boards set edgewise, and cause a lame ankle. The writer prefers good chestnut planks matched, and laid as above. The box stall is extremely comfortable, especially after a long ride, when the horse is warm and sweating freely, as he is likely to, on account of his thick coat of hair in winter. Warmth with good ventilation is conducive to health, and certainly to a good appearance, and the grain given under such conditions yields large returns. In a cold windy night, with the mercury at zero, such a stall with a good bed assures a comfortable rest, and is not beyond the means of any ordinary horse owner.

The hay should come from above and through a closed trough, and never be fed from a rack. The reaching up is very trying to the muscles of the neck and shoulders, and the constant scattering of the hay-seed and chaff into the horse's foretop and mane is alike irritating to the horse and his owner. If fed through a small opening in the bottom of a closed trough all this is avoided. The small opening also discourages wasting the hay, a trick which many horses have, and a costly one it is, for many a horse will waste more than he eats. The manger for the grain and other feed should be about eight inches wide and deep, and as long as the stall is wide. A hole or ring in the upper right hand corner will furnish a place for hitching. A heap of sand or sawdust should always be kept, with which to sprinkle the stable floor. If the horse's feet are dry, standing on the wet sand will help them, and when mixed with the urine and manure, it renders the fumes less volatile. A heap of dry earth or swamp muck should be kept under the barn, and every day or two a little thrown on the manure heap will prevent the heating so common to horse manure, and the consequent odors so fatal to harness polish and carriage varnish. The manure can and should be frequently removed. Sawdust is highly recommended by some horsemen, and it certainly changes the odor in and around the stable, but by others it is said to injure the horse's feet. Sand is to be preferred, but in the writer's experience no injurious results have ever been noticed.

The best bedding is doubtless rye-straw. It has a tougher fiber than oat or wheat straw, lasts longer and dries more readily. Enough should be used to make a good thick bed. If the horse is inclined to eat the bedding—a habit caused by lack of hay—the bedding that has been once dried should be put under the fore-feet and the new straw further back. It is a mistake under any circumstances to use wet straw, simply for economy's sake. Use new if the old is not dry, till it can be put in the sun, and if more is used than is needed some can be laid aside and used later. It does not require the exercise of much judgment to understand that when a horse, warm and tired, lies down on a mass of cold, wet and sometimes half decayed straw, rheumatism may naturally result, yet in the winter and rainy weather of spring the writer has often seen such bedding used. No animal better repays good treatment than the horse, and a good night's sleep on a dry bed is little enough to give after a hard day's work in the field, or a long drive on the road. To those living in the neighborhood of woods, leaves gathered in the fall when they are dry furnish a good bed, make a valuable addition to the manure heap, and of course cost practically nothing, as the children are always glad to spend part of a day in getting them. But they must be removed every day, as they cannot be dried. If oat or wheat straw is raised on the place, they should, of course, be used, subject to the same conditions as the rye straw.

FEEDING.

It is to be presumed that in the proper feeding of any horse, a fair amount of good sweet hay is almost a necessity. This need not always be the highest priced, but should never be dirty or musty.

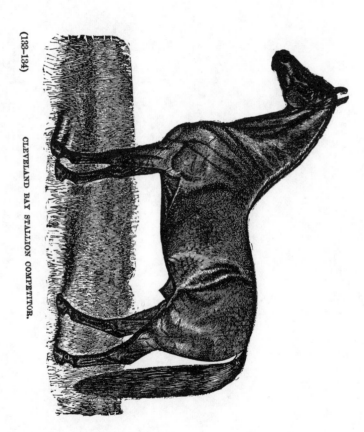

(133-134)

CLEVELAND BAY STALLION COMPETITOR.

Hay containing some clover is relished by most horses, and is good for them, promoting a healthy action of the bowels. Hungarian grass, well cured, is excellent, and if cut before the grain is matured there is nothing better. Oat straw, or oats cut when in the milk, are used by many farmers, but are very apt to be picked over by the horse and the larger part of them wasted. The uneaten part can be used for bedding, but the habit is soon acquired by the horse of picking out of all fodder what he likes best and leaving the rest, hence it is best to feed only what will be eaten up clean. Corn fodder is usually relished, and especially the green corn stalks, from which the ears have been taken for the table. A horse whose appetite is poor, or which is out of condition from hard work or other general causes, will be benefited more by a good feed twice a day of such stalks than anything the writer has ever seen, and a comparison in weight shows a constant gain during the feeding. There is hardly an animal that will not leave the best hay or grain for them, if all three are put in the manger together. Horses are partial to sweets, as most people know, and the carbonaceous matter contained in the juice of the stalks is very fattening.

The grain fed should be varied. A steady use of any particular kind is not good practice. An alternation of corn, whole or cracked, (or on the ear if one has it), Indian meal, oats, and provender can be made so that the horse will not tire of either. Cut hay, with meal or provender, makes a good feed once a day, though there is a disposition on the part of the horse to do less chewing than is sometimes necessary. Oats for the driving horse are reckoned by nearly all horsemen to be the best feed, but the eagerness with which some hungry horses eat them results in their being swallowed whole, and in this state they pass along the alimentary canal undigested, and are very often so found in the manure. Many of the second quality oats have no grain in the hull, and hence are not easily crushed by the teeth. In both these cases no possible benefit is derived from them. There is no better way of feeding oats than to grind them coarsely with a varying amount of sound Indian corn, some preferring equal quantities of each, and others two parts oats to one of corn. This coarse crushing renders both more easily digestible, and the corn furnishes the elements lacking in the oats. The so-called "provender" to be bought at the grain stores, consisting of second quality corn and oats, mixed often with middlings or shorts, does not count beside the real article. Cob-meal is fast losing its supporters, and has probably seen its best days. Roots—such as carrots, especially mangolds, or sugar beets, are doubtless nutritious and beneficial, some holding that carrots are worth as much as an equal weight of corn. They should be fed judiciously when available. The amount of grain to be fed should vary from six to ten quarts, according to the work done and the requirements of the horse. The idea prevalent among many horse owners, that a large animal needs an amount of feed proportional to his size and weight, is erroneous. The writer's horse, weighing eleven hundred and ten, keeps fatter, and in better condition every way, on six quarts of grain a day and seventy pounds of hay a week, than does the horse of a friend, weighing only eight hundred, on a larger quantity of both.

All the fresh water desired by the horse should be given, except when too warm, but always before eating. By the examination of a horse's receiving stomach it is shown to be much too small to hold an ordinary meal of grain and hay, and a pail or more of water after it. Hence, when the water enters, some of the food must be forced out undigested. A French horseman, in order to prove this point to some doubting friends, fed three horses with a kind of coarse bean of which they were fond, and as soon afterward as they would drink gave them all they wished. In less than half an hour afterward they were killed, and some of the beans, whole, partly chewed, and finely ground, were found in the intestines, fifteen feet from the stomach, where they had been carried by the water. It is a common practice for some good horsemen, at night, when they think the horse has finished eating, to go to the barn and give a pail of water, which will almost invariably be taken by the horse. Many a case of colic, fatal in some cases, had its origin, pure and simple, in the water given after the supper. No water should ever be given in less than an hour after the meal is ended, and two hours are twice as good an occasion. It is better, when possible, to feed the hay before the grain, for if either is to enter the bowels undigested it is much better to have hay there. A lump of rock salt should, of course, be a part of the stable outfit.

Before the morning meal, and, unless sweaty, before that of the evening, the horse should be well groomed. With a curry-comb, card, or corn-broom brush, rub the hair the wrong way till the dirt and dandruff are started from the skin, then with a brush or bunch of split cane rub till the glistening of the hair shows that the dirt is removed. An old woolen cloth or a piece of old carpet will complete the operation. The use of an ordinary house broom which has been about half worn out will be found very efficacious in cleaning the legs, and in fact the whole body. The mane and tail should be occasionally washed out, and, of course, brushed out daily. The tail ought always to be tied up where there is mud, or melted ice, or snow on the ground. Rubber coverings, in cold stormy weather, except

to a horse that is not driven rapidly, are comfortable, but they induce sweating, and so are best for horses that are not pushed as to
speed.   If the legs are wiped dry whenever the horse comes in wet,
and especially when there is snow or ice-water, the common disease,
scratches, will have less chance of making its appearance.   The
horse's feet should be cleaned whenever he stands all day in his
stall, and no manure should be allowed to accumulate on which he
can stand.   Absolute cleanliness is the price of healthy feet, a fact
which many learn too late, but which all good horse owners entirely
agree upon.

SHOEING.

The legs and feet of the horse are his weakest points, and nothing is more important to their well being than good shoeing.   That
the ordinary blacksmith or horse shoer knows absolutely nothing of
the structure of the foot can be soon ascertained by any one who will
ask the ordinary workman a half a dozen questions.   Mr. Russell, in
the lecture before spoken of, describes the English methods, which
he made the subject of personal observation in their best shops, as
"utterly irrational."   The shoes have a thick wide web, with high
calks at the heels only, lifting the horse's feet as some of the fashionable so-called French heels lift the over-dressed woman.   In both
cases, easy or comfortable traveling is out of the question.   The fact
that some English horses, whose names are known all over the
world and whose value is reckoned by the thousands of pounds, are
shod in this senseless way, shows plainly that their owners trust too
blindly to those who do not know their business.

In America we have, perhaps, as good shoeing as the world
affords, because horse owners have compelled the horse shoers to do
as they wished.   We have light, strong, well-made shoes, freedom
from the high calks, except in icy weather, when they are necessary.
Our chief fault is having the shoe fitted hot, or burnt into the hoof,
instead of having it put on absolutely cold throughout the whole
process of shoeing.   If any man who buys his shoes ready made
were to go into a store and try on a pair that did not fit him at all, and
should be told by the attending salesman that the shoes were "just
right," and should insist on his buying them on the plea that "the
foot would finally adapt itself to the shape of the shoe," the man
would think him a lunatic, and seek another place at once, where
the foot was of the first importance, and a shoe would be found to
fit.   But the first is in reality what is done when the horse is taken
to be shod.   A set of shoes is found with which it is decided to fit
the foot, or rather to make the foot fit, and then the farce or tragedy

begins. After some heating and pounding, and pressing the almost red-hot shoe against the already brittle hoof, after cutting away the heels, and trimming the frog as much as possibly can be done, the shoe is nailed on with eight large nails—six are always enough—and the horse is led away to suffer till the next shoeing.

The intelligent owner of a good horse should insist on the shoes being fitted cold, and of such size and shape as exactly fit the foot; that the heel is left open its natural width, and kept as low as the rest of the foot; that the frog be never cut, only trimmed where the edges are ragged, and the shape and condition of the foot remain as nearly natural as possible. If these conditions were insisted on, different work and workmen would be the result, and instead of the present stand-still for half a century or more, we should see improvement in the care of horses' feet; for Nature has done her part, and needs only to have man help her withstand the action of pavements and stony roads. What we need is a smith who will shoe a horse—as an artist once replied when asked, by an ignorant man, how he mixed his colors—"with brains, sir." A false idea of economy should not result in leaving the shoes on as long as they will stay. Once a month the feet should be examined by the smith, and his judgment should settle the question of new shoes. If he be a good reliable man, who sees in the interest of his customer his own, he will not make unnecessary expense.

CLIPPING THE HORSE.

"Should the family horse be clipped?" we hear some exclaim in surprise and horror, who, perhaps, have yielded a willing assent to all previous conditions, but we reply "Yes," in all candor and sincerity. Not in November or December, just for "looks" or "style," and no account taken of the days and nights when the mercury stands at zero—we do not wonder that in Ohio, that State of good horses, it is made an offense against statute law to clip a horse during the winter months—but in the spring, say the first or second week in April, or if the weather is mild and open, and the horse has begun to shed freely, the last week in March may do. Then to take off the old coat, to save all the currying and rubbing, to save the constant brushing of the clothes and carriage robes to free them from the flying hairs, to stop at once all the itching of the horse as the new hair begins to start, this is a mercy alike to the horse and his owner. That the horse is really more comfortable no one can doubt who gives it a thought, and it is a bit of personal experience which the writer would recommend to all horse owners, and especially to those who have no hostler or man servant to whom can be left the anything but agreeable task of cleaning a shedding horse. In three weeks the new hair will all be out, and a cleaner, sleeker animal it will be hard to find. The danger of taking cold is almost nothing, if ordinary precautions are taken.

BLANKETING.

The question of blanketing the horse has been a subject of controversy for several years. So far as the winter exposure goes, the blanket has been beneficial, and is steadily used—a thick, warm one for winter, a lighter one for spring and autumn, and a burlap covering for use during the day, while standing in the stall, as a protection against flies. It is urged by some that use of the blanket makes the horse tender and more liable to take cold, and also that nature will take care of the heat of the animal by furnishing an extra thick coat of hair; but we must remember that the horse, shut up in a barn more or less warm, does not conform to the same conditions as the wild animal, and that since the horse's appearance—a smooth, sleek coat is always gratifying to the owner—he must be careful that the horse is kept comfortable, without calling on nature more than is necessary. What would apply to horses used in the Maine pine forests to haul logs would not be proper for the horse kept for family use.

DOCTORING.

Horses are always liable to be sick, and some general directions would not, perhaps, be out of place here. In winter, colds are quite common throughout the Eastern and Middle States. If difficulty of breathing is noticed, with running at the nose, see first of all, that there are no drafts of cold air striking him; put on an extra blanket; give a warm bran mash and ten drops tincture of aconite once in two hours. If the cold take the form of a cough, there is nothing better than a tablespoonful of ground lobelia and ginger, mixed in equal parts, put in the bran mash, and it will be taken without trouble. Where the horse becomes suddenly lame, the first step is to ascertain whether or not it is the fault of the shoeing, as it very often is. In such a case, pull off the shoe, give the foot a rest of a day, and then put it on rightly. If it be due to a sprain, bathe in hot water and rub dry. The various liniments are not efficacious as a rule, and generally result in taking off the hair. It is better to call a well-known veterinary physician than to risk the loss of a valuable animal. The horse may die, of course, in spite of all that is done; but it will be a satisfaction in case of his death to feel that all has been done that was possible.

CHAPTER XIII.

VIEWS OF A VETERAN.

BY A. B. ALLEN.

THE STABLE.

THE best material for building a stable for the horse is brick, laid up with hollow walls; the inside one then prevents injurious dampness, and renders the atmosphere cooler in summer and warmer in winter. The next best walls are matched boards fastened on outside of the studs, then covered with strong thick paper made expressly for this purpose, and a second covering over it of matched boards, shingles, siding, or clapboards, as preferred. Stone walls are the coolest, and perhaps the most comfortable in summer, but the objection to them is, that they retain so much cold and dampness in winter as to chill the atmosphere, and render the horse liable to stiffness of limbs or rheumatism, although it may be warmly blanketed over its whole body. Slate is an excellent material for covering walls, and is growing in use, possessing nearly the same merits as brick. It is much better for roofing than shingles, being fireproof, lasts indefinitely, and costs but little more in many places. It is quite superior to tin or zinc. A roomy box stall is far preferable to the narrow kind, as it allows the horse to turn round and exercise at pleasure, which is quite important when not taken out for use during the day, and especially for several days in succession. This should be made of plank—oak is the best—at least an inch and a half thick, nailed to the inside of strong studs; then the lower plank cannot be pressed off by the horse placing his feet against it when getting up from lying down, nor the upper ones by the heavy leaning of his body. The plank should be perfectly sound, free from knots and cracks, and planed smooth, then if the horse rubs his tail or mane here it will not wear off the hair. The stall is best to extend north and south as near as possible, and the lower end open to the south side of the stable wall, in which set a large window to admit light behind the horse, instead of in front, to the probable injury of his sight. In addition to this, great benefit will be derived from the window in cold weather by letting in the sun to warm and dry the stable. In summer, shade it with a Venetian blind, which, by darkening the stable, also assists in keeping out flies. Fix the window to slide along the side of the stable, then it can be opened to any extent desired for ventilation. Additional ventilation may be necessary, especially when the weather is too cold to open the window. This is easily obtained by nailing four boards together, enclosing a space of six or more inches, and fasten this near the wall, with the lower end one or two feet above the stable floor, running it up through the roof and two or three feet above it. Over this set a cover a foot higher to keep out rain and snow. This ventilator draws in the foul air near the floor, and dissipates it above the roof, allowing pure air to take its place. The decided benefit of such a ventilator is, that it neutralizes drafts, and guards the horse from taking cold when the outside air is raw or very chilly. If one is not sufficient to do this, another may be added, in which case place them a few feet apart in the stall. It is cheaper to put in all such arrangements when the barn is being built than to add them later.

THE MANGER.

The manger should be set at the north end of the stall, boarding up near to it sufficiently high from the floor, and long and wide enough to hold a suitable ration of hay. Some prefer a rack set on a level with the head of the horse. This should never be higher, as it is unnatural for the horse, and sometimes, perhaps, painful and likely to get seed in his eyes as he reaches up to pull out his hay. An iron rack is generally preferable to one of wood.

THE FLOOR.

Sand is the best substance for the floor of the stall, and it is drier and more elastic than other soil for the feet to rest on. Plank or wooden blocks are next best. Cement becomes slippery, and if a little wet it is difficult for the horse to get up after lying down, for there is nothing on it to assist his feet. Moreover, it is harder than plank, and more trying to the feet and legs. Stone is not to be thought of, it is too hard and rough. These floors should be abundantly littered. Peat moss, as now pressed in bales and sold in market, is most approved, as it is soft and elastic, absorbs fluids quickly, and fixes ammonia in a superior manner ; thus neutralizing all unpleasant smell and injuriousness to the eyes, and adds value to the manure heap. It has the further merit that it can be dried and used several times more than other kinds of litter. Straw, salt meadow and marsh hay make excellent bedding ; but it is advisable to pass these through the fodder cutter before using them, for when shortened from full length the horse cannot so well paw the litter into heaps under it. It also mixes more evenly with the droppings, causing less fermentation and heating in the manure heap. It is more conveniently handled with the dung fork and shovel, and it decomposes more rapidly when applied to crops. Seaweed makes excellent litter, while sawdust and clear sand answer tolerably. Some recommend common earth, but it becomes muddy when wet, and badly soils the horse, and makes it uncomfortable. A gutter in the stable floor in rear of the horse is unnecessary to carry off the urine, where plenty of litter is used, as this absorbs and saves about all the salts, and it is an ugly thing for the horse to step in.

STORAGE OF MANURE.

A good method for keeping manure is to lay a cement or plank floor at a convenient distance from the stable, with a water-tight rim raised a few inches all around. Cover this with a roof sufficiently high for a man to stand under when the pile is finished. Haul out the manure as fast as made in the stable, and dump it here in even layers about six inches deep, and let it lie till wanted for the crops. No drainage can come from this, and to prevent loss of ammonia, scatter plaster of Paris about half an inch thick over every layer as fast as made. This, aside from fixing the ammonia, will add more than its cost to the value of the manure. If there is any danger of firing, a little peat, muck, turf, or good soil spread over each layer will prevent it. But when the land is tolerably level, so that drainage from it cannot run off, there is no necessity of storing manure, at least from early autumn till late in spring, as it may be carted as fast as made and spread broadcast on meadows and fields to be cultivated for the next season's crop. The little waste of ammonia in the air from this exposure is more than compensated by the manure getting well rotted, and covering the ground during winter. This is the cheapest way to dispose of manure, as it is only once handled, and the work is performed mainly in winter, when there is little else to do. Manure may be kept in the open air also with little loss in heaps, by first spreading hay, straw or seaweed a foot thick on the ground, and piling the manure over this as it is taken from the stable. The thick underlayer preserves the salts washed down by the rain or melted snow, as I have proved by frequent trials, and these two last assist in nicely rotting it by spring. Some let their manure accumulate and lie on the stable floor all winter; but this makes so soft and damp a bed for the horse to stand on, as to become injurious to the hoofs, and, although spread out evenly and well littered, there will be a more or less offensive and unhealthy smell from it, particularly in warm days. Others dump through a trap door into a cellar under the stable, which is still more objectionable, though muck and litter may be mixed up with it, and swine kept there to root over and trample the layers.

WATERING AND GROOMING.

Water the horse in the morning before feeding, otherwise it might wash more or less of the food just eaten undigested from the stomach. The water should be blood-warm in cold weather, but it may be less so when mild. Never give water icy cold, as it might produce chills or colic. After standing a few minutes let the horse first eat a little hay, and then give the grain or meal ration. Now remove the blanket and groom the horse, scratching lightly with the curry-comb, followed by a brush that penetrates well through the hair to the skin, until nicely cleaned. Use a comb with long coarse teeth to the mane, passing it through from the under side; then the hair is not pulled out or shortened on the top. Use this comb also for the tail, in addition to which the top may require to be brushed, but do this carefully so as not to pull out or rub off any of the hair. A long full tail is a great beauty to a horse. If one prefer, the legs and pasterns may be rubbed with wisps of straw or hay instead of the curry-comb and brush. Finish by cleaning the feet.

FODDER.

Hay for feeding horses is most esteemed in the Northern and Eastern States, made from grasses in the following order: Timothy, herds grass or red-top, orchard grass, ray grass; and both Alsike and red clover. The two latter are best grown mixed with the above grasses. If grown and fed alone, they must be free from dust, otherwise it might be injurious to the health of the horse. All should be cut in full blossom, and cured as much as possible in the swath, windrow, or cock, as this best retains their sweetness and tenderness. The Kentucky blue-grass is highly valuable where it grows freely, and many prefer it to all other grasses for hay. Every one of the above makes excellent pasture.

In the valleys and on the vast plains east and west of the Rocky Mountains, several very nutritious species of grass grow naturally, alike excellent for pasture and hay. Alfalfa or Lucern grown there gives three to four heavy cuttings during the season, under proper irrigation, but it must be fed with caution when green, for fear of colic. All Eastern grasses may also be freely grown there. At the South, Japan clover is most highly prized, and next follow Bermuda grass and Johnson grass, while a few grasses natural to the country and elsewhere are more or less esteemed. Northern cultivated grasses and the millets are also successfully grown there in different sections.

At both the North and South, oats, wheat, rye and barley are useful for pasture before getting too rank ; and cut when the grain is in the milk, just before it begins to harden, and properly cured, these make excellent hay, more especially the oats. Corn-stalks are best grown of the sweet dwarf sorts, in rows two to three feet apart, and the stalks standing about three inches apart in the rows. They are sweeter then and far more nutritious than grown up thickly from the seed sown broadcast. Cut when 'n the silk or a nubbin begins to form, and properly cured, my horses greedily eat the whole from butt to tassel, and often prefer them to choicest hay when both lay side by side.

GRAIN AND MEAL.

Oats and barley are preferred as horse feed in the order named, and are best ground. Corn alone is too fattening, and occasionally gives colic. It should be ground and fed about half and half mixed with wheat bran. Some think unbolted wheat and rye flour are superior to this mixture, and if found too rich or heavy, a little pure bran may be added to them to increase that already left in the ground grain. To each of the above half a pint to a pint of linseed or oil meal may be added night and morning. This promotes digestion, slightly lubricates the intestines, and causes a better relishing of the other food. At the South, cotton-seed meal takes the place of this, but it occasionally affects Northern animals unfavorably, and must therefore be fed cautiously. Hay passed short through the fodder cutter to the amount of a peck or half a bushel, with the meal ration mixed in it, and then wet up, is often fed twice to thrice a day in addition to long hay; but this occasionally causes severe colic to the horse. When ascertained, change this ration to hay and meal dry, each by itself. A few quarts of roots per day, when no other green food is given, are highly beneficial, as they soften and promote the digestion of the dry food. Carrots are the best, sugar beets and mangels next. Parsnips, I know not how truly, are said to affect the eyes ; yet I do not see how this should be. Potatoes and turnips, unless cooked, are apt to bring on scours.

SALT, ASHES, AND SULPHUR.

Keep constantly a good-sized lump of rock-salt in the feed-box for the horse to nibble at pleasure. It will then take just as much as its appetite craves, and no more than is needful. Give a heaping tablespoonful of clean wood-ashes twice a week in the meal ration, and the same quantity of sulphur two or three times per month, as all these are conducive to health, and serve to ward off disease.

PASTURE.

If the horse is not employed at extra fast or hard work, it is best to pasture it when convenient through the growing weather, unless flies and mosquitoes are quite annoying ; then it should be stabled during the day and turned out during the night. If the grass is abundant and of a good quality, the horse will eat enough during this time to support it well, with the addition of hay and a few quarts of meal at noon in the stable, which ought to be moderately darkened to keep out the flies. See that the horse has access to plenty of pure water in the pasture.

THE TEETH.

Examine the horse's back teeth occasionally, and see that none have grown up longer than others. If so, the horse cannot masticate its food properly, and they must be filed down to a level with the rest. Files are made expressly for this purpose. Also look for decayed teeth, and if found extract them. If lampas is formed, feed a little hard corn, and the mastication of it will soon wear this off. The corn may at first give some soreness to the gums ; if so, stop it a few days until relieved, and then feed again. This is considered much better than lancing, and nothing like so barbarous and painful to the horse as burning with a red-hot iron, as is sometimes done. Lampas is merely a congested condition, not a disease.

RIDING AND DRIVING.

When the horse is taken out for either riding or driving, it should not be allowed to move at a fast pace for the first mile or more, otherwise, as its stomach is then full, it may injure its wind and bring on the heaves. A good rule to observe before putting the horse up to a fast gait is to let it dung three times. This relieves the bowels to a moderate extent. If necessary to stop when out, and a cold wind prevails, put the horse under cover and blanket ; if one is not to be had then hitch on the lee side of some building. If in summer, put in a shade as clear from flies and mosquitoes as possible ; if there is no net cover with a cotton sheet or light blanket. The best strap for hitching is one that buckles round the neck, as it holds more securely than a halter or bridle rein, which are liable to be slipped.

In crossing a river or bay in a steamboat or other conveyance in cold weather, or facing a raw or strong wind on the road, hang a short thick blanket from the neck spread in full breadth over the chest, to guard from taking cold. When the exposure ceases, remove it. Returning home from a ride or drive of some extent, and the horse is sweaty, let the last mile be done slowly that it may be cooled a little before reaching the stable. Some blanket as soon as the harness is taken off ; others contend that it is better to rub as dry as possible and then blanket. But which may be preferable will depend something on the weather and the nature of the horse, whether to dry quickly, or to sweat longer and copiously. If the feet and legs are muddy, again, some prefer to let it dry on before cleaning, and then it is easily rubbed off ; others wash it off immediately. The objection to this in cold weather is, that the groom is apt to neglect wiping perfectly dry after the washing, and in consequence stiffness of the limbs or rheumatism may follow.

Examine the shoes, and if gravel or any hard substance has got between them and the hoofs, pick it out. During this time, the horse may safely take two to four quarts of water, at a moderate temperature if in summer, and warmer if in winter. After being well cooled give all the water the horse will drink. Now wait a short time and then feed a little hay at first, after which his ration of grain or meal. Never let a horse stand or wade in water when he is hot, as it would endanger foundering him unless the water is quite warm, and perhaps even then. If ever forced to do this, exercise him well after it, and when stabled, rub the legs thoroughly dry down to the hoofs, then he would probably escape founder ; but if danger still exists, bandage the legs in thick woolen cloths, and keep them on as long as necessary.

SHOEING.

Do not let shoes remain on the horse's feet over three to six weeks, dependent on the amount of use and the toughness and growth of the hoofs. Each time after taking off the shoes, if the road permits, let him go barefoot as long as no injury follows, as this expands the hoofs and keeps them in more perfect condition. Some horses can be used barefoot, off pavements, for months, or the whole year round, and work better than if shod. Never allow the frog of the foot to be cut out or trimmed, unless somewhat ragged, and then only a very little, as it acts as a cushion to the foot and lessens or even prevents bruising when striking a stone or other hard substance. See that the hoof is not pared beyond absolute necessity, and that the shoe is properly fitted to it, and not the hoof to the shoe. Do not allow the bottom of the hoof to be burnt or even scorched with a hot shoe, in order to make it set evenly, but pare it properly to do so.

THE HARNESS AND SADDLE.

Keep the harness well oiled and supple, and when either that or the saddle is put on the horse, see that it fits nicely, and does not chafe any part of the body or limbs. In winter be careful to warm the bridle bit before using it, otherwise it might be frosty enough to freeze to the inside of the mouth, and stick long enough to blister it and the tongue badly. Never permit a check rein on the harness bridle to be hooked up tight as drivers will persist in doing ; it gives the horse great pain, especially when standing, as all may observe from seeing him constantly tossing his head up and down, and one side to the other, seeking relief from the cruel torment. In addition to this, it soon makes a hard mouth, and when moving along, and especially while ascending a hill, the horse cannot stretch out his head and neck as is necessary for him in order to use his full strength to move the load more easily to which he is attached.

BLINDERS.

The use of the blinders is a pernicious custom. If a horse is broken to harness as he should be without them, there never will be any necessity of wearing them. They are injurious to the eyes and the vision, and it is as absurd to use them in harness as it would be under the saddle. The horse is much more liable to shy, jump, rear, and even run, with blinders, than without them. Having had horses with all these tricks in my possession, I changed the bridle for one without blinders, and they soon ceased their capers; for they could then fully see all objects on both sides in gradually approaching them, as well as in front, and thus were not troubled or scared. The best harness-broken horses I found in my travels abroad were in Russia, and they wore no blinders. I never saw even those of the highest spirit either shy, jump, rear, or attempt to run. In driving out, teach the horse to stop instantly at the word "whoa," especially in descending a hill. If the harness then, or anything about the carriage, should give way, this would prevent its crowding against the horse or cause him to be frightened.

CONCLUSION.

The horse is the noblest, the most beautiful, and the most useful of all our domestic animals. Without this faithful servant, it is doubtful whether any people could reach a high state of civilization. It behooves us then to treat him with the greatest kindness and consideration. Never speak roughly but always gently to him; and when approached, pat him gently on the body and neck, and stroke his face down soothingly with the hand. This will insure his confidence in you, strict obedience, and marked affection. Quite vicious horses have often been subdued by kindness alone, and made safe to be handled and used; still, there is a risk, and for a family horse it is advisable to choose such only as are of a gentle natural disposition, and free from all kinds of vice and tricks.

CHAPTER XIV.

THE FAMILY HORSE IN THE PRAIRIE STATES.

BY FRED GRUNDY, ILLINOIS.

SELECTING THE HORSE.

In buying a "family horse" choose one rather short and compactly built, broad between the eyes and ears, with regular, straight face, wide, thin nostrils and mild, intelligent, pleasant eyes. Such an animal will be safe, kind, reliable, and attached to its master and home. It will not travel so fast as a long, slim, leggy horse, but will do more work on less feed. Avoid the slim, tucked-up, bony animal with legs like a greyhound, ears sharply cocked, and flashing eyes, as also the elephantine lubberly corn crib. Both may be useful in their spheres, but they are not suitable for "family" horses. The villager, trucker, small farmer, or suburban resident who needs a horse only a portion of the season, or a part of each day during the whole season, will find it advantageous to buy a sound, strong, well-built mare, breed her to a good horse and raise a colt each year. It will require but little more time to care for both than for one. The mare will be unfit for driving or work only a short time, and this can be arranged to come at a convenient season, and the colt will much more than pay the cost. Of course this cannot be done in all cases, but the suggestion is worthy of serious consideration. For about two months previous to foaling, the mare should not be driven at more than a moderate gait, nor very far in one day. Care should be taken that she is not worked or driven until very hot or tired, nor exposed to cold rains. Good oats, bran and hay form the best feed for her, and she should have sufficient of these to supply all demands on her system. Her condition is the feeder's best guide, keep her in good flesh—not fat. Give her at least two weeks' liberty and rest after foaling. Carrots and green feed will increase the flow of milk. It is not necessary that the colt run with her all the time. Two or three-hour drives can be made without injury to either. After it has learned to eat and drink, separation for half a day at a time is rather beneficial than otherwise.

TREATMENT.

Treat the horse kindly at all times. Teach it to stand still until told to go. When you wish it to stop short say "whoa!" and never at any other time. If going too fast, say "steady." Speak plainly and act sensibly, and it will understand what is wanted and be prompt to obey.

STABLE.

In building a stable it is much the best plan to make a good one. It need not be made of expensive materials, but should be well put together. The foundation should be of stone or brick, solidly laid. The frame should be of sound timbers. Cover the frame with common rough boards, these with tarred or plain building paper carefully joined to close all chinks, and over all good barn siding, well nailed on and battened. The rafters should be closely covered with common boards, then tarred paper, and finished with the best shingles, and the whole building painted with two coats of mineral paint. Such a building will be warmer in winter and cooler in summer than one made of brick, and with occasional repainting will stand for generations. It should contain a good wide stall, harness room, two bins for feed, besides loft room for at least two tons of hay. The harness room and bins should be mouse-proof and be lighted by windows. The stall should be well lighted by a window placed either above the manger, or at one side, near the horse's head. All the windows should be fitted with screens to exclude flies, mice, etc., and arranged to be readily opened, much or little as desired, for ventilation. The floor of the stall may be of clay tamped solid, or of plank. Each has its advantages. A good clay floor is cooler than one of plank, and is said to be easier on the feet of a horse that is driven much on stony ground or paved streets. I prefer the clay floor because of its coolness. Have it about two inches lower at the rear.

For bedding, good wheat straw is best. Oat straw is too tough, and barley straw is irritating to the skin. Straw bedding will not absorb all the liquids nor prevent strong ammoniacal vapors from arising, and therefore absorbents of some sort should be kept on hand. Dry earth is best; plaster is good; sifted coal ashes and dry sawdust may be employed. A shovelful of either will absorb the liquids, which are of high manurial value, and preserve them in a much safer, more compact and portable form than can be done in a filthy cistern. By the use of dry earth or any other good absorbent the stable can be kept perfectly clean and sweet at all times, and a shovelful can be scattered over the floor as quickly as a forkful of straw. A dry stall and dry bedding are essential to the comfort and health of the horse.

Connected with the stable should be a well-drained yard for the horse to exercise in whenever it is not in use. A gate arranged so that it can be slid forward to inclose the stable door within the yard is a good contrivance. With a sliding door for the stall, the horse can be turned loose and given the run of both yard and stall. For brood mares this is an excellent arrangement—much better than a box stall or shedded yard. If the yard can be enlarged to a small pasture so much the better. Sow it with Kentucky blue grass, orchard grass and timothy, equal quantities of each, by weight, at the rate of two bushels per acre. Use no clover, because its second growth causes salivation. The horse should have some exercise every day if possible. Continued enforced idleness is very injurious. The muscles become soft, the flesh flabby, the system clogged, and he is soon rendered unfit for even light work. A moderate amount of exercise will prevent this, and keep the animal in good condition for hard work and long drives.

GROOMING.

Thorough grooming is as essential to the health, comfort and appearance of the horse as proper food and shelter. Curry and brush it from head to foot at least once every day. Use the comb lightly and the brush vigorously. Aim to make the operation agreeable to the horse. When it comes in wet and muddy, wash its legs and feet clean with warm water and rub dry with a cloth; it will prevent scratches and other like ailments. In warm weather sponge off the shoulders, and other parts sweated by the harness, with cool, salty water, then wipe dry. If the horse should accidentally become galled, use the following ointment: Clean lard, two ounces, acetate of copper one-quarter ounce, Venice turpentine one-half ounce, spirits turpentine one-half ounce. Melt slowly and mix, and stir till cold. Carefully wash the galls twice a day, dry with cloth, and apply the ointment. Let the animal rest until healed.

SHOEING.

Keep the hoofs nicely rounded off smooth. Unless driven largely over pavement or stony roads it is best not to have the horse shod. The feet will remain sounder and it will travel all ordinary roads better without. If the roads are stony or slippery it is best to have shoes. Have the shoe fitted to the foot, not the foot to the shoe. See that the shoe is neither too thick nor too heavy. There is little danger of its being too light. Have the hoof surface perfectly flat, and the shoe fitted close up, to prevent gravel from working in between the sole and the shoe. In no case allow the frog to be reduced farther than the removal of the ragged ends. If it comes in contact with the ground when the shoe is on, so much the better— it was made to come in contact with the ground and relieve the shock to the shoulder, and it should be let alone. Opening the heels is also injurious to the foot, and should never be allowed. Young horses require shoeing more frequently than old. Shoe as often as is necessary to preserve the symmetry of the foot. Horses that wear their shoes unevenly will, if in constant use, require shoeing once a month, and it is best not to allow one set of shoes to remain on any horse over two months at the longest.

GROWING PART OF THE FEED.

Quite a large quantity of feed can be grown on a small lot. Cut oats when just ripe, bind in small sheaves, allow to stand in small shocks until the straw is cured, then store away in the hay mow to be fed out in the bundle during the winter months. They form an agreeable variety, and a horse will eat them, straw and all, with a relish. After the oats, early potatoes and other vegetables are harvested, the ground may be sown to millet, which in a fair season will make a large quantity of green feed. It should all be cut and fed or converted into hay before seed forms. After the millet is harvested the ground may be plowed and sown to rye, which will be ready to cut for green feed in the spring long before anything else. If the land is not needed for other crops, follow the rye with oats and the oats with millet. If the soil is kept moderately rich, a good crop of each is almost a certainty. With this rotation an immense quantity of green and dry horse-feed can be cheaply grown on a small patch of land, and there will be no chance for weeds. However small the lot some carrots should be grown, to be stored in the cellar for feeding in winter and early spring. For this purpose the Half-long Stump-rooted is best, as they grow to a good size, yield heavily, and are not difficult to harvest. It rarely pays to grow corn for horse feed on a small lot. Immature corn, either green or cured, is not good food for horses.

FEEDING.

In this matter no rigid rule is applicable. Some horses require nearly twice as much feed as others of equal size to keep in equally good condition. The owner of a horse must determine how much feed is required by intelligent experiment, and the condition of the animal must be the guide. It is no sign that a horse has not had sufficient because the manger is found empty. Feed a horse lightly when at rest—just enough to keep in good condition. Increase the feed when at work, not a day or two previous as is the common practice. Clean, bright, early cut hay is best for a working horse. Experience has proved that it rarely pays to run it through a feed cutter. All hay that is dusty should be dampened slightly when fed. Heaves are caused by feeding overripe and dusty hay, or by driving rapidly on a full stomach. Heaves is an incurable disease, always caused by mismanagement, and it depreciates the value of a horse fully one-half. An animal afflicted with this disease can be comfortably driven and worked on such feed as carrots, oats soaked in water six hours, and grass or bright oat straw dampened. Equal weights of oats and corn, whole or ground, forms an excellent grain feed for horses. Two parts oats, two of bran, and one of shelled corn, if slightly dampened, is also very good for a working animal. All overripe or moldy hay, and moldy or damaged grain of all sorts are not only worthless for feed, but also extremely injurious to the animal. Carefully avoid all such trash. The value of carrots for feeding in winter, and in early spring when the horse is shedding its coat, cannot be overestimated. They act on the digestive organs similar to grass, keeping the bowels open and the system cool when the animal is on dry feed. One or two carrots may be cut fine and mixed with the evening meal. An hour on pasture every evening in summer is excellent. If this cannot be had, an armful of green grass is the next best. Green millet with a little bright oat straw and the regular grain ration make a very good feed for evenings in late summer. A horse lightly worked will winter nicely on clean oat straw, with a mixed ration of oats, bran, shelled corn and carrots twice a day. Horses worked hard and steadily should have the best of hay. It is the poorest kind of economy to buy cheap feed of any sort.

INDEX.

DESCRIPTIVE CATALOGUE

—OF—

RURAL BOOKS,

CONTAINING 116 8vo. PAGES,

PROFUSELY ILLUSTRATED, AND GIVING FULL DESCRIPTIONS OF
NEARLY 600 WORKS ON THE FOLLOWING SUBJECTS·

Farm and Garden,

Fruits, Flowers, Etc.

Cattle, Sheep, and Swine,

Dogs, Horses, Riding, Etc.,

Poultry, Pigeons, and Bees,

Angling and Fishing,

Boating, Canoeing, and Sailing,

Field Sports and Natural History,

Hunting, Shooting, Etc.,

Architecture and Building,

Landscape Gardening,

Household and Miscellaneous.

PUBLISHERS AND IMPORTERS:

ORANGE JUDD COMPANY,

52 & 54 Lafayette Place, New York.

Books will be Forwarded, postpaid, on receipt of Price.

Mushrooms: How to Grow Them.

Any one who has an ordinary house cellar, woodshed or barn, can grow Mushrooms. This is the most practical work on the subject ever written, and the only book on growing Mushrooms published in America. The author describes how he grows Mushrooms, and how they are grown for profit by the leading market gardeners, and for home use by the most successful private growers. Engravings drawn from nature expressly for this work. By Wm. Falconer. Cloth. Price, postpaid.   1.50

Land Draining.

A Handbook for Farmers on the Principles and Practice of Draining, by Manly Miles, giving the results of his extended experience in laying tile drains. The directions for the laying out and the construction of tile drains will enable the farmer to avoid the errors of imperfect construction, and the disappointment that must necessarily follow. This manual for practical farmers will also be found convenient for references in regard to many questions that may arise in crop growing, aside from the special subjects of drainage of which it treats. Cloth, 12mo.   1.00

Allen's New American Farm Book.

The very best work on the subject; comprising all that can be condensed into an available volume. Originally by Richard L. Allen. Revised and greatly enlarged by Lewis F. Allen. Cloth, 12mo. 2.50

Henderson's Gardening for Profit.

By Peter Henderson. The standard work on Market and Family Gardening. The successful experience of the author for more than thirty years, and his willingness to tell, as he does in this work, the secret of his success for the benefit of others, enables him to give most valuable information. The book is profusely illustrated. Cloth, 12mo.   2.00

Henderson's Gardening for Pleasure.

A guide to the amateur in the fruit, vegetable and flower garden, with full descriptions for the greenhouse, conservatory and window garden. It meets the wants of all classes in country, city and village who keep a garden for their own enjoyment rather than for the sale of products. By Peter Henderson. Finely Illustrated. Cloth, 12mo.   2.00

Johnson's How Crops Grow.

New Edition. A Treatise on the Chemical Composition, Structure and Life of the Plant. Revised Edition. This book is a guide to the knowledge of agricultural plants, their composition, their structure and modes of development and growth; of the complex organizations of plants, and the use of the parts; the germination of seeds, and the food of plants obtained both from the air and the soil. The book is a valuable one to all real students of agriculture. With numerous illustrations and tables of analysis. By Prof. Samuel W. Johnson of Yale College. Cloth, 12mo.   2.00

Johnson's How Crops Feed.

A Treatise on the Atmosphere and the Soil, as related in the Nutrition of Agricultural Plants. This volume—the companion and complement to "How Crops Grow"—has been welcomed by those who appreciate the scientific aspects of agriculture. Illustrated. By Prof. Samuel W. Johnson. Cloth, 12mo.   2.00

Market Gardening and Farm Notes.

By Barnet Landreth. Experiences and Observations for both North and South, of interest to the Amateur Gardener, Trucker and Farmer. A novel feature of the book is the calendar of farm and garden operations for each month of the year; the chapters on fertilizers, transplanting, succession and rotation of crops, the packing, shipping and marketing of vegetables, will be especially useful to market gardeners. Cloth, 12mo.   1.00

Forest Planting.

A Treatise on the Care of Woodlands and the Restoration of the Denuded Timber-Lands on Plains and Mountains. By H. Nicholas Jarchow, LL. D. The author has fully described those European methods which have proved to be most useful in maintaining the superb forests of the old world. This experience has been adapted to the different climates and trees of America, full instructions being given for forest planting on our various kinds of soil and subsoil, whether on mountain or valley. Illustrated, 12mo.   1.50

Harris' Talks on Manures.

By Joseph Harris, M. S., author of "Walks and Talks on the Farm," "Harris on the Pig," etc. Revised and enlarged by the author. A series of familiar and practical talks between the author and the Deacon, the Doctor, and other neighbors, on the whole subject of manures and fertilizers; including a chapter especially written for it, by Sir John Bennet Lawes of Rothamsted, England. Cloth, 12mo.   1.75

Truck Farming at the South.

A work which gives the experience of a successful grower of vegetables or "truck" for Northern markets. Essential to any one who contemplates entering this promising field of Agriculture. By A. Oemler of Georgia. Illustrated, cloth, 12mo.   1.50

Sweet Potato Culture.

Giving full instructions from starting the plants to harvesting and storing the crop. With a chapter on the Chinese Yam. By James Fitz, Keswich, Va., author of "Southern Apple and Peach Culture." Cloth, 12mo.   .60

Heinrich's Window Flower Garden.

The author is a practical florist, and this enterprising volume embodies his personal experiences in Window Gardening during a long period. New and enlarged edition. By Julius J. Heinrich. Fully illustrated. Cloth, 12mo.   .75

Greenhouse Construction.

By Prof. L. R. Taft. A complete treatise on Greenhouse structures and arrangements of the various forms and styles of Plant Houses for professional florists as well as amateurs. All the best and most approved structures are so fully and clearly described that anyone who desires to build a Greenhouse will have no difficulty in determining the kind best suited to his purpose. The modern and most successful methods of heating and ventilating are fully treated upon. Special chapters are devoted to houses used for the growing of one kind of plants exclusively. The construction of hotbeds and frames receives appropriate attention. Over one hundred excellent illustrations, specially engraved for this work, make every point clear to the reader and add considerably to the artistic appearance of the book. Cloth, 12mo.   1.50

Bulbs and Tuberous-Rooted Plants.

By C. L. Allen. A complete treatise on the History, Description, Methods of Propagation and full Directions for the successful culture of Bulbs in the garden, Dwelling and Greenhouse. As generally treated, bulbs are an expensive luxury, while, when properly managed, they afford the greatest amount of pleasure at the least cost. The author of this book has for many years made bulb growing a specialty, and is a recognized authority on their cultivation and management. The illustrations which embellish this work have been drawn from nature, and have been engraved especially for this book. The cultural directions are plainly stated, practical and to the point. Cloth, 12mo.   2.00

Henderson's Practical Floriculture.

By Peter Henderson. A guide to the successful propagation and cultivation of florists' plants. The work is not one for florists and gardeners only, but the amateur's wants are constantly kept in mind, and we have a very complete treatise on the cultivation of flowers under glass, or in the open air, suited to those who grow flowers for pleasure as well as those who make them a matter of trade. Beautifully illustrated. New and enlarged edition. Cloth, 12mo.   1.50

Long's Ornamental Gardening for Americans.

A Treatise on Beautifying Homes, Rural Districts and Cemeteries. A plain and practical work at a moderate price, with numerous illustrations and instructions so plain that they may be readily followed. By Elias A. Long, Landscape Architect. Illustrated, Cloth, 12mo.   2.00

The Propagation of Plants.

By Andrew S. Fuller. Illustrated with numerous engravings. An eminently practical and useful work. Describing the process of hybridizing and crossing species and varieties, and also the many different modes by which cultivated plants may be propagated and multiplied. Cloth, 12mo.   1.50